Sports and Athletics Preparation, Performance, and Psychology

SPORT-SPECIFIC STRENGTH TRAINING: BACKGROUND, RATIONALE, AND PROGRAM

SPORTS AND ATHLETICS PREPARATION, PERFORMANCE, AND PSYCHOLOGY

Is Sports Nutrition for Sale? Ethical Issues and Professional Concerns for Exercise Physiologists
William T. Boone (Author)
2005. 1-59454-422-0

Doping in Sports
Christopher N. Burns (Editor)
1-59454-683-5

Literature Reviews in Sport Psychology
Sheldon Hanton and Stephen Mellalieu (Authors)
2006. 1-59454-904-4

Hot Topics in Sports and Athletics
Samuel R. Bakere (Editor)
2008. 978-1-60456-077-0

Sports Injuries and their Effects on Health
Robert R. Salerno (Editor)
2009. 978-1-60741-507-7

A Competitive Anxiety Review: Recent Directions in Sport Psychology Research
Stephen D. Mellalieu, Sheldon Hanton and David Fletcher (Authors)
2009. 978-1-60692-248-4

Former NFL Players: Disabilities, Benefits, and Related Issues
Thomas P. Wasser (Editor)
2009. 978-1-60692-346-7

Thoroughbred Horseracing and the Welfare of the Thoroughbred
Cameron L. Stratton (Editor)
2009. 978-1-60692-724-3

Advances in Strength and Conditioning Research
Michael Duncan and Mark Lyons (Editors)
2009. 978-1-60692-909-4

Contemporary Sport Psychology
Robert Schinke (Editor)
2009. 978-1-60876-150-0

Handbook of Sports Psychology
Calvin H. Chang (Editor)
2009. 978-1-60741-256-4

Strength Training: Types and Principles, Benefits and Concerns
James T. Kai (Author)
2009. 978-1-60876-221-7

A Competitive Anxiety Review: Recent Directions in Sport Psychology Research
Stephen D. Mellalieu, Sheldon Hanton and David Fletcher (Authors)
2009. 978-1-60876-405-1

Advances in Strength and Conditioning Research
Michael Duncan and Mark Lyons (Editors)
2009. 978-1-60876-661-1

Aerobic Exercise and Athletic Performance: Types, Duration and Health Benefits
David C. Lieberman (Editor)
2010. 978-1-60876-217-0

Advancements in the Scientific Study of Combative Sports
Jason E. Warnick and W. Daniel Martin (Editors)
2010. 978-1-60876-733-5

Aerobic Exercise in Special Populations
Carlos Ayan Perez , Jose Maria Cancela Carral and Silvia Varela Martinez (Authors)
2010. 978-1-60876-697-0

Sport-Specific Strength Training:
Background, Rationale, and Program
Del P. Wong, Michael A. Tse, June Lee-chuen Chin and Christopher Carling (Authors)
2010. 978-1-61668-259-0

World Book of Swimming: From Science to Performance
Ludovic Seifert and Didier Chollet (Editors)
2010. 978-1-61668-202-6

Sport-Specific Strength Training: Background, Rationale, and Program
Del P. Wong, Michael A. Tse, June Lee-chuen Chin and Christopher Carling (Authors)
2010. 978-1-61668-600-0

Trends in Human Performance Research
Michael J. Duncan and Mark Lyons (Editors)
2010. 978-1-61668-591-1

Trends in Human Performance Research
Michael J. Duncan and Mark Lyons (Editors)
2010. 978-1-61728-086-3

Sports and Athletics Preparation, Performance, and Psychology

SPORT-SPECIFIC STRENGTH TRAINING: BACKGROUND, RATIONALE, AND PROGRAM

DEL P. WONG
MICHAEL A. TSE
JUNE LEE-CHUEN CHIN
AND
CHRISTOPHER CARLING

Nova Science Publishers, Inc.
New York

Library of Congress Cataloging-in-Publication Data

Available upon Request

ISBN: 978-1-61668-259-0

Published by Nova Science Publishers, Inc. † New York

CONTENTS

PREFACE

This chapter aims to review the latest scientific research in the application and design of sport-specific strength training programmes in three types of sport: a team sport (soccer), a racket sport (badminton) and a water sport (rowing). Generally, training programs designed to improve sports performance involve metabolic training (i.e., aerobic or anaerobic metabolism), functional training (i.e., training to enhance movement), and strength training (i.e., training to enhance muscle capacity). In this chapter, we will focus on the strength training regimes specific to soccer, badminton, and rowing. In each sport, we will consider the: 1) physical demands of competition, 2) anthropometry/body type suitable for the sport, 3) body movements, muscle recruitment and range of motion of the sport. In addition, the 4) modalities of training exercise, 5) periodization, and 6) common injuries and their prevention in each sport will be also covered. With the aforementioned information, we will show the rationales behind the sport specific strength training programs, and lastly we will illustrate some samples of strength training programmes.

Chapter 1

1. SOCCER

1.1. PHYSIOLOGY AND BIOMECHANICS OF SOCCER

1.1.1. Physical Requirements for Soccer

Soccer involves two teams of 11 players who attempt to propel the ball through a set of goals, while preventing the opposition team from doing the same. The game consists of two 45 minute halves, with a 15 minute rest between halves. Players at elite levels have to run ~ 10 to 12 kilometers during a game depending on their playing position (Di Salvo et al., 2007; Rampinini, Coutts, Castagna, Sassi, & Impellizzeri, 2007), and exercise intensity is close to the anaerobic threshold, i.e., 80 - 90% of maximal heart rate (Stolen, Chamari, Castagna, & Wisloff, 2005). In addition, exercise intensity is reduced and distance covered is 5 - 10% less in the second half compared to the first half (Mohr, Krustrup, & Bangsbo, 2003; Rienzi, Drust, Reilly, Carter, & Martin, 2000; Wong, Chamari, Moalla et al., In press) and players run less distances at high speeds towards the end of the game (Bradley *et al.*, 2009). In general, approximately 98% of total energy expenditure is derived from the aerobic metabolism (Stolen et al., 2005).

Numerous explosive activities are also required in soccer, such as jumping, kicking, tackling, turning, sprinting, and changing pace (Carling, Bloomfield, Nelsen, & Reilly, 2008). These explosive activities required high levels of strength, power, speed, and agility. Specifically, a sprint bout occurs approximately every 90 seconds in competition, each lasting an average of 2 to 4 seconds (Reilly & Thomas, 1976), while sprinting constitutes 1 to 11% of the total distance covered during competition (Di Salvo et al., 2007).

Therefore, analysis of soccer game demonstrates periods and situations requiring high-intensity activity during which there is accumulation of muscle lactate leading to transient fatigue (Stolen et al., 2005).

1.1.2. Physical Characteristics

Soccer players are assigned to different positions in which they perform various tactical and technical tasks. In analyses of soccer, positions are generally classed into 5 separate roles including the goalkeeper, central defenders (centre-back), external defenders (full-backs), central midfielders, external midfielders (wing), and forwards (Di Salvo et al., 2007; Rampinini et al., 2007). There are substantial differences in anthropometric and physiological characteristics across playing positions (Carling, Reilly, & Williams, 2008). For example, a recent study analyzed FIFA World Cup players and reported significant differences in anthropometric measures between players across the positions: goalkeepers were the heaviest and tallest, while midfielders were the lightest and shortest (Wong *et al.*, 2008). Therefore, it is believed that anthropometric characteristics contribute to success in specific playing positions at the senior level. For example, taller and heavier players are more suitable for the roles of goalkeeper and defender, whereas shorter and lighter players are more suitable to a midfield role. Nevertheless, some modern midfielders who were taller than average for this position have also been successful at the highest level.

Other than the anthropometric aspect, various physical activity profiles exist in different playing positions (Carling, Bloomfield et al., 2008; Stolen et al., 2005). Previous studies on professional match-play have shown that forwards cover the greatest distance (~ 3000 meters) in high speed activities (Di Salvo et al., 2007; Rampinini et al., 2007). In contrast, central midfielders cover the a greater total distance (~ 12000 meters) throughout the match, and also undertake the highest number of dribbling attempts (Di Salvo et al., 2007). In addition, work by Reilly et al. (2000) has shown that midfielders have the highest maximal oxygen uptake among elite senior soccer players. Therefore, it is believed that intermittent running endurance and aerobic capacity are important for achieving success in a midfield role. On the other hand, central defenders cover less total distance compared to other outfield players but make a greater number of actions where they head the ball (Carling, Williams, & Reilly, 2005). The activity profile of goalkeepers is not as great as that of outfield players but the high intensity actions carried out by players in this position are often highly decisive in the final result of competition. In this regard, a previous study reported data showing that elite goalkeepers cover a distance of 5611 meters during professional competition, with an average sprint length of ~ 11 meters (Di Salvo, Benito, Calderon, Di Salvo, & Pigozz, 2008). In addition, the goalkeepers walked for a total of 73% of the match duration, whereas 2% of match time was spent at high intensity (Di Salvo et al., 2008).

With regard to young soccer players, a previous study investigating anthropometric characteristics in elite players of ~ 14 years of age reported significant differences across positional roles (Carling, Le Gall, Reilly, & Williams, 2009; Reilly et al., 2000; Wong, Chamari, Dellal, & Wisloff, In press). Research by Reilly et al. (2000) on elite youth players showed that forwards were significantly lighter than goalkeepers, defenders, and midfielders; significantly shorter than goalkeepers, defenders, and midfielders; and had significantly lower body mass index compared to defenders. However, no significant positional differences were observed in their physiological performances such as maximal vertical jump height, ball-shooting speed, 10 meters and 30 meter sprint times, Yo-Yo Intermittent Endurance Run, running cost, sub-maximal heart rate, maximal oxygen uptake, and maximal heart rate (Wong, Chamari, Dellal et al., In press). A related study in elite U/14 French youth players also reported no difference in fitness measures between playing positions in players who eventually turned professional compared to players who remained amateur (Le Gall, Carling, Williams, & Reilly, In press,). Therefore, positional differences across some physiological and anthropometric characteristics may not have sufficiently developed in young soccer players who have < 5 yrs of intensive soccer training experience (Malina, Eisenmann, Cumming, Ribeiro, & Aroso, 2004; Wong, Chamari, Dellal et al., In press).

1.1.3. Body Movements, Muscle Recruitment and Range of Motion

A wide range of skills form the basis of soccer play but kicking and shooting are the most widely studied skills (Lees & Nolan, 1998). The kicking and shooting movements are similar and characterized by an approach to the ball using one or more strides, with placement of the supporting foot at the side of and slightly behind the stationary ball. The kicking leg is first drawn backwards and the leg flexed at the knee. Forward motion is initiated by rotating the pelvis around the supporting leg and by bringing the thigh of the kicking leg forwards while the knee continues to flex. Once this initial action has taken place, the thigh begins to decelerate until it is essentially motionless at ball contact. During this deceleration phase, the shank vigorously extends about the knee to almost full extension at ball contact. The leg remains straight through ball contact and begins to flex during the long follow-through. The foot often reaches above the level of the hip during the follow-through (Lees & Nolan, 1998).

During soccer kicking and shooting, the joint moment is greatest at the hip joint and least at the ankle joint. Furthermore, greater muscle moments were generated about the hip joint (280 Nm), followed by the knee joint (140 Nm), and finally about the ankle joint (30 Nm) (Lees & Nolan, 1998). Moreover, strength of knee flexors ($r = 0.77$), knee extensors ($r = 0.74$), hip flexors ($r = 0.56$) and hip extensors ($r = 0.56$) are reported as being significantly correlated to kicking performance (Lees & Nolan, 1998). Specifically, the iliopsoas, rectus femoris, vastus lateralis, vastus medialis, biceps femoris, gluteus maximus, semitendinosus, and tibialis anterior are all considered as major muscles involved in kicking and shooting (Kellis & Katis, 2007). Although the strength in these muscles is crucial, the coordination of joint segments and timing of muscle action are also important to kicking performance (Carling, Reilly et al., 2008; Lees & Nolan, 1998). In this regard, the speed of kicking can be increased by ~ 20 % when using a stretch-shortening action rather than a purely concentric muscular contraction to extend the knee joint. Specifically, the thigh is brought forward while the knee is still flexing. Such actions stretch the knee extensor before they are required to shorten, so that higher speed is generated to bring the shank towards the ball (Lees & Nolan, 1998).

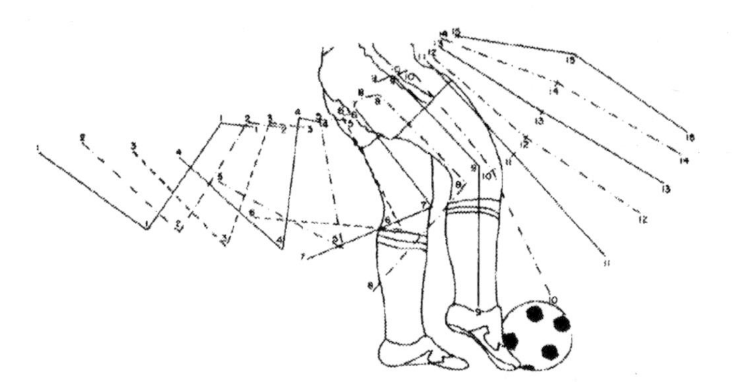

Figure 1. Range of motion during kicking and shooting. Picture modified from Plagenhoef (1971).

With regard to the range of motion during kicking and shooting (Figure 1), the backswing phase involves the backward movement of the kicking leg, with the hip extending up to ~29^0, the knee is flexed up to ~ 45^0 and the ankle being plantarflexed to 10^0 (Kellis & Katis, 2007; Lees & Nolan, 1998). During forward motion, the kicking leg forwards with the hip starts to flex (hip angle at 20^0), while the knee continues to flex, and the ankle is plantarflexed. Upon impact, the hip is flexed, the knee is slightly flexed at 30^0, and the ankle is plantarflexed (Kellis & Katis, 2007; Lees & Nolan, 1998).

1.2. Soccer Specific Strength Training Programs

1.2.1. Modalities of Training Exercise

Strength is required in many aspects of soccer play but particularly in contact situations against opponents for control of the ball. Successful performance during explosive activities in soccer such as turning, sprinting and changing pace can be improved by increasing the available force from muscular contraction in appropriate muscle groups (Hoff & Helgerud, 2004). Many studies have investigated the effects of muscular strength training on soccer performance (Gorostiaga et al., 2004; Hoff, 2005; Kotzamanidis, Chatzopoulos, Michailidis, Papaiakovou, & Patikas, 2005; Manolopoulos, Papadopoulos, Salonikidis, Katartzi, & Poluha, 2004; Nunez, Da Silva-Grigoletto, Castillo, Poblador, & Lancho, 2008 ; Ronnestad, Kvamme, Sunde, & Raastad, 2008). For example, increased muscular strength is reported to improve jump height, rate of force development, running economy and 10 meters, 20 meters, and 40 meters sprint times (Hoff & Helgerud, 2004). Moreover, it has been reported that jump height ($r = 0.78$), 10 meters ($r = 0.94$) and 30 meters ($r = 0.71$) sprint performance are highly correlated with maximal muscular strength (Wisloff, Castagna, Helgerud, Jones, & Hoff, 2004). Additionally, combining strength training and power training improves explosive performance and power-related skills to a greater extent than any of the two training modalities alone (Fatouros *et al.*, 2000). Furthermore, strength training exercises at high movement speeds are recommended in order to improve explosive soccer performance (Wong & Wong, in press).

Muscular strength can be increased by two mechanisms: muscular hypertrophy and neural adaptation (Hoff & Helgerud, 2004). The former increases the cross-sectional area of muscle and results in greater body mass, which is generally not desirable in soccer because players will have to move with a heavier body. In contrast, neural adaptations enhance muscle strength by recruiting more muscle fibres and causing minimal increase in body mass (Hoff & Helgerud, 2004). Therefore, in order to maximize strength gain without an increase in body mass, conditioning programmes for soccer players that already have sufficient muscle mass should use training sets based on high loads and short repetitions (i.e., 4 – 6 Repetition Maximum) for 3 – 4 sets (Hoff & Helgerud, 2004) with 2 – 5 minutes rest in-between sets (Baechle, Earle, & Wathen, 2000).

As aforementioned, it is important to improve soccer players' strength and power capacity while maintaining an appropriate level of aerobic endurance. In addition, it is of great concern to soccer coaches that such a strength training program may induce negative effects on aerobic endurance. To concurrently improve and/or maintain the aerobic endurance, prolonged continuous running exercise has been traditionally used (Jones & Carter, 2000; Mikesell & Dudley, 1983) but this kind of exercise relies mainly on the fat metabolism, which is not specific to the intermittent and high-intensity activity patterns in soccer that require both fat and carbohydrate oxidation (Stolen et al., 2005). Specifically, it has been shown that during 90 minutes of intermittent exercise, fat oxidation was almost 3 times lower and carbohydrate oxidation was ~ 1.2 times higher, compared to continuous exercise with the same overall energy expenditure (Christmass, Dawson, Passeretto, & Arthur, 1999). Recently, a high-intensity intermittent/interval training regime was developed for players to cope with the specific physical requirements of professional soccer. In this context, Dupont, Akakpo, and Berthoin (2004) combined repeated-sprint efforts (12 x 40 meters, with 30 seconds passive rest) and high-intensity interval runs (120% of maximal aerobic speed for 15 seconds, alternated with 15 seconds passive rest for 12 to 15 intervals) once per week for 10 weeks during the in-season in a group of professional soccer players. Results showed a significant improvement in both 40 meters sprint time and maximal aerobic speed.

Docherty and Sporer (2000) proposed an interference model for concurrent muscular strength training and aerobic endurance training. The authors stated that muscle hypertrophy-type training combined with high-intensity aerobic interval training, has the greatest interference effect. Specifically, hypertrophy-type strength training increases contractile protein, but has negative effect on mitochondrial density and the oxidative enzymes which subsequently inhibits aerobic endurance (Bishop, Jenkins, Mackinnon,

McEniery, & Carey, 1999; Sale, Macdougall, Jacobs, & Garner, 1990). In addition, continuous aerobic endurance training increases the mitochondrial content, oxidative capacity, and converts muscle fibre characteristics from fast to slow twitch, which affect the development of explosive performance (Putman, Xu, Gillies, MacLean, & Bell, 2004). In contrast, a muscular strength programme using high loads ranging from 3 – 6 Repetition Maximum combined with a high-intensity interval training regime, reduces the interference effect. This is due to the effects of muscular strength training which stresses the neural system and does not place metabolic demands (i.e., protein synthesis) on the working muscles. Consequently, the muscle can increase its oxidative capability as a training response to aerobic interval training without affecting neural adaptation, thus improving aerobic endurance. Therefore, the use of high loads in strength and power training combined with high-intensity interval running to achieve optimal training effects on both explosive performance and aerobic endurance in soccer players is recommended (Wong, Chaouachi, Chamari, Dellal, & Wisloff, In press).

1.2.2. Periodization

The use of prolonged high-intensity training is risky if recovery is insufficient and can lead to over-reaching or over-training with a concomitant decrease in performances (A. Coutts, Reaburn, Piva, & Murphy, 2007; Halson & Jeukendrup, 2004). Moreover, it has been reported that a higher incidence of illness and reduction in salivary immunoglobulin levels were associated with increased workload without sufficient recovery among women soccer players (Putlur *et al.*, 2004). Therefore, the yearly training plan of a soccer team requires appropriate periods for training and recovery so that improvement in performance is possible (Gamble, 2006; Rowbottom, 2000; Woodman & Pyke, 1991).

The following phases are common in the planning of soccer fitness regimes. These include: pre-season preparation, in-season competition, and off-season recovery (Kelly & Coutts, 2007; Woodman & Pyke, 1991). Training load is gradually progressive throughout the pre-season preparatory period (Rowbottom, 2000) and players undertake a period of rest or taper prior to competition (A. J. Coutts, Reaburn, Piva, & Rowsell, 2007; Mujika & Padilla, 2003). With respect to strength training, intensity and volume are both high in the pre-season preparation phase in which a limited amount of sport-specific skill training is employed (Wathen, Baechel, & Earle, 2000). During this phase, strength training can lead to high levels of fatigue as well as requiring a large commitment in time, and sport performance will not be at peak levels. After the pre-season preparation phase, training volume is subsequently decreased and intensity is increased in the pre-season specific preparation phase (Wathen et al., 2000). In this phase, strength training is sport-specific, and the volume of strength training is decreased in order to increase the involvement of sport-specific skill training. The volume of strength training is further decreased in the pre-competition phase so that the training of skills (technique and tactical) is optimized and maximized (Wathen et al., 2000). There are various types of tapering technique used for professional team sports in this phase (Bosquet, Montpetit, Arvisais, & Mujika, 2007; Mujika, 1998; Mujika & Padilla, 2003).

High intensity (> 90% of 1 Repetition Maximum) and very low volume (1 - 3 sets of 1 - 3 repetitions) strength training is performed during the in-season competition phase depending on the competitive fixtures to maintain strength level in players (Wathen et al., 2000). The majority of training time in this phase is devoted to sport-specific skill training and recovery in order to achieve peak performance (Wathen *et al.*, 2000). During the season in particular, the weekly periodization of high-intensity training activity affects the team performance during competition (Owen, Wong, & Chamari, In press). It has been shown that the minimal volume of high-intensity training (defined as the duration of performing training activities that are > 85% of individual maximal heart rate) is performed 2 days preceding competition in professional soccer teams (Owen et al., In press). In addition, this work showed that players received one day-off after the match. In comparison to those weeks with no match, the weekly high intensity volume was reduced: 27% and 67% respectively for weeks with 1 match and 2 matches. The volume of high-intensity training was reduced gradually from the beginning of the season to the 20th week in order to spare energy for competition and avoid any unfavorable fatigue (Owen et al., In press).

1.2.3. Common Injuries and Prevention

Soccer play is generally associated with a high risk of injury. Most soccer injuries are shown to occur in the lower extremities (Hawkins & Fuller, 1999; Wong & Hong, 2005). The ankle joint is especially prone to injury because it is close to the ball and is also the focus during soccer activities such as dribbling, shooting and tackling (Wong & Hong, 2005; Woods, Hawkins,

Hulse, & Hodson, 2003). In addition, the upper leg and groin are also among the most commonly injured body parts, possibly because of the large muscle mass and the large area exposed (Junge & Dvorak, 2004). The most common injury mechanics are tackling, running, shooting, twisting and turning, jumping and landing. In addition, a higher injury rate during elite competition has been observed as compared with training, possibly due to higher intensity of play in competition (Wong & Hong, 2005). Furthermore, professional players generally have a higher overall injury rate and in competition than adolescent players (Wong & Hong, 2005). Finally, elite players who had sustained a previous injury (Hägglund, Waldén, & Ekstrand, 2006) and had decreased range of motion (Arnason *et al.*, 2004) were more at risk of injury.

Previous studies have proposed several methods to reduce the risk of and prevent soccer injuries. These include: a warm-up with more emphasis on stretching; regular cool-down; sufficient recovery time between training; proprioceptive training; protective equipment; and good playing field conditions (Junge, Rosch, Peterson, Graf-Baumann, & Dvorak, 2002). With respect to training, it has been shown that an adequate pre-season conditioning programme resulted in 2.5 less injury incidence as compared with no training group (Heidt, Sweeterman, Carlonas, Traub, & Tekulve, 2000). Furthermore, Junge et al. (2002) reported that an intervention program designed to improve the stability of ankle and knee joints, flexibility and power of the trunk, hip and leg muscles, resulted in 21% fewer injuries during one soccer season. Moreover, training the dynamic stability of the ankle joint using an inflatable disk and unstable surface has demonstrated a positive effect on injury prevention (Cressey, West, Tiberio, Kraemer, & Maresh, 2007; Tropp, Askling, & Gillguist, 1985).

1.2.4. Age Issues – Junior/Youth

The intensity of competition played by young soccer players is different to that reported in senior players. Specifically, game intensity decreases with age and match level which are indicated by the distance coverage (professional senior: ~11 kilometers; U18: ~9 kilometers; and U12: ~6.2 kilometers in 60 minutes 11-a-side match), heart rate response (professional senior: 93% of maximal heart rate; U18: 82% of maximal heart rate), and blood lactate concentration (professional senior: 10 $mmol \cdot L^{-1}$; and U12: 5 $mmol \cdot L^{-1}$) (Capranica, Tessitore, Guidetti, & Figura, 2001; Castagna, D'Ottavio, & Abt, 2003; Di Salvo et al., 2007; Helgerud, Engen, Wisloff, & Hoff, 2001;

Rampinini et al., 2007; Stolen et al., 2005). Furthermore, it has been reported to takes ~10 years of training and competition for young soccer players to achieve elite level ability (Helsen, Hodges, Van Winckel, & Starkes, 2000). Young soccer players play at lower intensities and have shorter match duration as compared to senior players, thus the specific physiological characteristics are not fully not developed at younger age levels (Wong, Chamari, Dellal et al., In press). Furthermore, research in elite youth players has demonstrated that high performance in fitness measures at a younger age may not always be associated with achieving success later on (Carling et al., 2009). Therefore, soccer and conditioning programs should be adapted to the current physical and mental capacities of youth soccer players as the programmes used by senior players are not appropriate.

1.2.5. Strength Training Program Samples

In this section, samples of strength training programmes in different phases are illustrated. It is recommended that a fully qualified and certified strength and conditioning specialists supervise the strength training session to ensure proper technique and safety. The following programs are based on previous studies and modified to suit professional and youth soccer players, respectively (Baechle et al., 2000; Potach & Chu, 2000; Wong, Chamari, & Wisloff, In press; Wong, Chaouachi et al., In press). The program for professional senior players (Figure 2) is performed in a straight-set (i.e one exercise after another) for 4 sets each with 6 Repetition Maximum and ~ 3 minutes rest between sets to maximise strength gains by neural adaptation (Baechle et al., 2000). This type of strength training has been reported to induce minor muscular hypertrophy (Kyrolainen *et al.*, 2005) and did not interfere with the development of aerobic endurance (Paavolainen, Hakkinen, Hamalainen, Nummela, & Rusko, 1999; Wong, Chaouachi et al., In press). Plyometric exercises are also included to further improve explosive performances (Fatouros *et al.*, 2000). In addition to these exercises, players performed sit-up exercises for core-strengthening.

The programme for adolescent/youth players (Figure 3) is performed without heavy external weight to avoid placing strain on the immature or developing skeleton musculature. Instead, the programme includes plyometric exercises that stimulate the stretch-shortening cycle of the musculotendinous unit. It is believed that these exercises enhance agility, dynamic balance, and quickness in adolescent/youth players (Christou et al., 2006; Faigenbaum et al., 2007; Jullien et al., 2008; Kotzamanidis et al., 2005; Nunez et al., 2008 ; Ronnestad et al., 2008; Sheppard & Young, 2006).

Phase: Pre-season general preparation Duration: 3 times a week for 4 weeks'	
Exercise	Set x Intensity, Rest
Single-arm alternate-leg bound [plyo]	3 x 10Contact, 3min
Double-leg tuck jump [plyo]	3 x 6Rep, 3min
High-pull	4 x 6RM, 3min
Squat jump [p]	4 x 6RM, 3min
Bench press	4 x 6RM, 3min
Back half squat	4 x 6RM, 3min
Chin up/lat pull down	4 x 6RM, 3min
Sit-up	3 x 15Rep, 2min
Phase: Pre-season specific preparation Duration: 2 to 3 times a week for 4 weeks	
Exercise	Set x Intensity, Rest
Depth jump with lateral movement [plyo]	3 x 10contact, 3min
Double-leg pike jump [plyo]	3 x 6Rep, 3min
Power-clean [p]	4 x 6RM, 3min
Squat jump [p]	3 x 6RM, 3min
Bench press	3 x 6RM, 3min
Back half squat	3 x 6RM, 3min
Chin up/lat pull down	3 x 6RM, 3min
Plyometric sit-up [plyo]	3 x 15Rep of 4kg, 2min
Phase: In-season competition Duration: once a week	
Exercise	Set x Intensity, Rest
Depth jump with lateral movement [plyo]	3 x 10contact, 3min
Double-leg pike jump [plyo]	3 x 6Rep, 3min
Power-clean [p]	3 x 3RM, 3min
Squat jump [p]	3 x 3RM, 3min
Bench press	3 x 3RM, 3min
Back half squat	3 x 3RM, 3min
Chin up/lat pull down	3 x 3RM, 3min
Plyometric sit-up [plyo]	3 x 15Rep of 4kg, 2min

Note: RM = repetition maximum, Rep = repetition, p = power exercise; plyo = plyometric exercise.

Figure 2. Strength and conditioning program for professional senior players.

Phase: Pre-season general preparation Duration: 3 times a week for 4 weeks	
Exercise	Set x Intensity, Rest
Split squat jump plyo	3 x 6Rep, 3min
Single-arm alternate-leg bound plyo	3 x 10Contact, 3min
Double-leg tuck jump plyo	3 x 6Rep, 3min
Lateral hurdle hop plyo	3 x 10Rep, 3min
Walking lunge	4 x 10Rep, 3min
Push up	4 x 15Rep, 3min
Sit-up	3 x 15Rep, 2min
Phase: Pre-season specific preparation Duration: 2 to 3 times a week for 4 weeks	
Exercise	Set x Intensity, Rest
Cycled split squat jump plyo	3 x 6Rep, 3min
Double-arm alternate-leg bound plyo	3 x 10Contact, 3min
Double-leg pike jump plyo	3 x 6Rep, 3min
Jump over hurdle with lateral movement plyo	3 x 6Rep, 3min
Walking lunge	4 x 10Rep, 3min
Push up	4 x 15Rep, 3min
Plyometric sit-up plyo	3 x 12Rep of 2kg, 2min
Phase: In-season competition Duration: once a week	
Exercise	Set x Intensity, Rest
Cycled split squat jump plyo	2 x 6Rep, 3min
Double-arm alternate-leg bound plyo	3 x 10Contact, 3min
Double-leg pike jump plyo	2 x 6Rep, 3min
Jump over hurdle with lateral movement plyo	3 x 6Rep, 3min
Walking lunge	3 x 10Rep, 3min
Push up	3 x 12Rep, 3min
Plyometric sit-up plyo	2 x 10Rep of 2kg, 2min

Note: Rep = repetition, and plyo = plyometric exercise.

Figure 3. Strength and conditioning program for adolescent/youth players.

Chapter 2

2. BADMINTON

2.1. PHYSIOLOGY AND BIOMECHANICS OF BADMINTON

2.1.1. Physical Requirements of Badminton

Badminton is an intermittent sport played on a single court area of 20 x 17 feet and in which high intensity activities are interspersed with short rest pauses (Mills, 1977). The fitness requirements of professional badminton players include muscular strength, muscular endurance, agility, aerobic endurance, speed, balance, neuromuscular coordination (Pelton, 1971), flexibility (Liang, 1991), and stability (Hirakawa & Shogei, 1994). These physical skills are reflected in the actual demands of match-play. It has been reported that ~ 26 shots per minute were observed in the men's single final in the 1996 Olympics (United States Olympic Committee, 1998). Additionally, around 85% of the rallies ended within 1 - 10 seconds, and about 10% of rallies ended within 20 - 40 seconds during national competitions (Wang, 1995). In addition, the average length of the rallies and the duration of one men's single match were 4.57 - 8.86 seconds and ~ 25 minutes, respectively (Manrique & Gonzalez-Badillo, 2003). Previous research in international players has reported performance intervals of 6.4 seconds and rest time of 12.9 seconds between exchanges (Majumdar *et al.*, 1997). More recently, Faude et al. (2007) found that work density was approximately 0.51 (rally time divided by rest time) regardless of the event, i.e. mixed, singles or doubles.

Knowledge about the physiological demands in badminton competition provides the basis for evidence-based design of training regimens (Faude et al., 2007). Game analysis also provides information on the fatigue endured by players which is manifested by mistimed strokes, lower speed, and altered on-court movements (Girard & Millet, 2008). Indeed, an awareness of game characteristics, together with data on the correlations between certain actions such as unforced errors and winning shots and the final result of the match, will aid in more appropriate planning and monitoring of specific training (Manrique & Gonzalez-Badillo, 2003).

In this regard, it has been reported that values greater than 95% of maximal heart rate were recorded in badminton competition (Araragi, Omori, & Iwata, 1999; Faccini & Dal Monte, 1996), and the absolute heart rate values ranged from 186 to 201 beats·min^{-1} (Faccini & Dal Monte, 1996; Manrique & Gonzalez-Badillo, 2003). In international level players, these high demands have been confirmed as players recorded a maximum heart rate of 190.5 beats·min^{-1} and an average of 173.5 beats·min^{-1} during matches over 28 minutes long (Majumdar et al., 1997). Many overhead strokes are observed in badminton as compared with tennis which partly explains the elevated heart rates found in badminton (Reilly, 1990). Energy consumption has been reported as 46 – 52 ml·min·kg^{-1} (Faccini & Dal Monte, 1996; Faude et al., 2007) in male players, and 36 ml·min·kg^{-1} in female national players (Faude et al., 2007). These values correspond to 73 – 86 % of players' maximal oxygen uptake. In addition, blood lactate concentrations ranging from 0.9 – 5.1 mmol·L^{-1} were observed in a badminton match and a simulated match respectively (Faccini & Dal Monte, 1996; Faude et al., 2007; Manrique & Gonzalez-Badillo, 2003). The short bouts of high intensity activities are interspaced with recovery periods allowing ample opportunity for the oxidative metabolism to predominate. Therefore, the anaerobic by-products can be locally oxidized or transported from production site to oxidative muscle fibers for subsequent oxidation during exercise and recovery time (Faccini & Dal Monte, 1996). In other words, a well-developed aerobic capacity will enhance recovery during high intensity intermittent exercise (Tomlin & Wenger, 2001).

2.1.2. Physical Characteristics

Various tactical approaches have been adopted in different countries (Wang, 1995). For example, a combination of drop shots and smashes at the back of the court is used by European players in order to utilize their advantage in stature while fast and skillful attacks combined with high agility are observed in Asian players. In this regard, previous studies found that the body height of international male badminton players from European countries ranges from 1.79 – 1.86 meters (Andersen, Larsson, Overgaard, & Aagaard, 2007; Wonisch, Hofmann, Schwaberger, von Duvillard, & Klein, 2003).

The physical characteristics of the game have been affected by changes in the rules of the game. For instance, the Badminton World Federation changed the rules in 2006 leading to a game that is more explosive and played at a faster pace - placing great physiological strain on the players. The maximal oxygen uptake values of internationally ranked badminton men and women players are reported as ~ 62 $ml \cdot min \cdot kg^{-1}$ and 50 $ml \cdot min \cdot kg^{-1}$, respectively (Faude et al., 2007).

2.1.3. Body Movements, Muscle Recruitment and Range of Motion

In general, badminton involves some common movements such as running, jumping, throwing, reaching, stopping, and starting (Gambetta, 2007). Previous studies (B. C. Elliott, 2000; Lees, 2003; Rambely, Wan Abas, & Yusof, 2005; Waddell & Gowitzke, 2000) have described ball hitting movements in detail and the majority of investigations were conducted in tennis and squash (Bahamonde, 2000; B. C. Elliott, Marshall, & Noffal, 1995; Eygendaal, Rahussen, & Diercks, 2007; Mashall & Elliott, 2000; Sprigings, Marshall, Elliott, & Jennings, 1994). Furthermore, as all stroke movements in racket sports have a similar fundamental mechanical structure (B. Elliott, 2006), the analysis of movements in badminton is made with reference to other racket sports and to overhead throwing/hitting actions.

On court badminton skills can be categorized as overhead shots/smashes, shoulder height shots, underarm shots, and service (Roper, 1985). A movement unique to badminton is the upper body movement during overhead smash, which is the top scoring shot (~54%) among all attacking shots (Tong & Hong, 2000). Research by Waddell and Gowitzke (2000) has shown that a professional badminton player takes advantage of long resistance torque distances for rotational movements at both the shoulder and radio-ulnar joints in order to produce the power needed in the smash with a minimum energy cost. Furthermore, the energy transfer from proximal to distal joints is important in generating speed and power in shots. The smash movement is divided into three phases to facilitate analysis: preparatory (back swing), action, and recovery (or follow-through) (Lo & Stark, 1991). The Badminton smash is similar to an over-arm throwing movement that is characterized by lateral rotation of the humerus in the preparation phase and its medial rotation in the action phase (Bartllet, 2000). Specifically, these movements are accompanied by rotation of the pelvis and trunk in the opposite direction from the intended throw (rotating backward to the right side for right-hander), horizontal abduction, and lateral rotation at the shoulder joint with elbow flexion and wrist hyperextension (Hamilton, Weimar, & Luttgens, 2008).

The preparatory phase ends with the forward strike of the opposite leg. During the action phase, the elbow joint extension is followed by a rapid medial rotation at the shoulder joint, forearm pronation at the ulna-radius joint, and then ulnar flexion at the wrist joint (Hamilton *et al.*, 2008). The sequence of muscle recruitment is from proximal (large) muscle groups to distal (small) muscle groups. The accuracy of movement also increases through the recruitment of muscles with a progressively decreasing innervation ratio (Bartllet, 1999). The action phase is finished when the shuttlecock is hit and the final phase (recovery) involves the controlled deceleration of the movement by eccentric contraction of the appropriate muscles.

The body segments act as a system of chain links, whereby the force generated by one body segment can be transferred successively to the next link, and if a delay occurs between segments this reduces the stored energy. In this context, Elliott, Baxter, and Besier (1999) showed that movement velocity was significantly (20%) faster in a no-pause condition when compared with both short- and long-pause conditions. In a powerful stroke such as smash and clear, a number of body segments were involved and coordinated to produce the highest racket speed at impact (B. Elliott, 2006). To achieve this, the speed of each segment should be faster than that of its predecessor (Kreighbaum & Barthels, 1996). For example, energy is generated from the joints of the lower body and is then transferred to the trunk, shoulder joint, elbow joint, and wrist joint (Waddell & Gowitzke, 2000). In related research, Cheetham et al. (1998) found that professional golfers demonstrated superior energy transfer from proximal segments to distal segments as compared to amateur golfers. Hamilton et al. (2008) found that over-arm throwing patterns in inexperienced players are characterized by fewer segments involvement, working more simultaneously rather than sequentially, and involved less range of motion. Moreover, apart from the energy transfer from proximal to distal joints, long-axis rotation is also important in the development of speed in badminton movements. Therefore, the upper arm internal rotation and forearm pronation occurs late in racket sport movements such as tennis serve and squash forehand drive movements (Mashall & Elliott, 2000).

Lo and Stark (1991) analyzed the overhead shot and divided the skill into phases and found muscles in both arms (racket side and non-racket side), upper body, and lower body were involved. Therefore, almost all muscles are involved in this action: the major muscle groups of pectoralis, biceps and triceps, trapezius, and rhomboid for upper body; gluteus, quadriceps, hamstrings, and calves for lower body. Sakurai and Ohtsuki (2000) found that skilled players produced proper activation of upper body and arm muscles of the racket limb during a smash, whereas unskilled players produce wasted activity. Furthermore, research has found that the forearm supinated before rapid pronation to increase the speed of the movement in smash (Tang, Abe, Katon, & Ae, 1995). This pre-stretch movement takes advantage of the elastic properties of muscle and inherent proprioceptive reflexes. It works when the elastic fibers in the connective tissue shorten after the preceding stretch ceases. Likewise, it has been found that professional players who had high shuttle velocity, generate force from the preparatory phase and pre-stretch the knee extensors before immediate jumping (Tsai & Chang, 1998).

2.2. Badminton Specific Strength Training Programs

2.2.1. Modalities of Training Exercise

As mentioned previously, high performance badminton players require well-developed muscular strength/power, agility, aerobic and anaerobic metabolisms. In different training phases, coaches manipulate training variables in order to elicit optimal training stimulus. Concurrent training has been employed to address the two major physical skills needed for badminton: muscular strength/power and aerobic endurance (Bell, Syrotuik, Socha, Maclean, & Quinney, 1997; Chromiak & Mulvaney, 1990; Dudley & Fleck, 1987). During concurrent training, the muscle fibers face the dilemma of trying to adapt to the oxidative stimulus to improve aerobic function as well as adapting to the stimulus from a heavy resistance training program to improve force production ability (Fleck & Kraemer, 2004). Kraemer et al. (1995) showed a shift in muscle fiber types from Type IIB to type IIA in all the training groups, and indicated that when two high intensity training programs were used, with one focusing on high intensity strength, the adaptive response at muscle fiber level was not the same compared to when a single training mode was used. However, upper body strength was not affected by the lower body endurance training. This result implied that the training of two different muscle groups can be done concurrently.

Most studies have shown that strength was compromised with concurrent strength and aerobic endurance training, whereas aerobic endurance capability was not affected. Hennessy & Watson (1994) showed that strength and power capacity in professional players is more susceptible to this training method due to the simultaneous high intensity and volume of training. In contrast, a study by Rhea et al. (2008) demonstrated that power training and intense, lengthy aerobic endurance training are not compatible and resulted in decreased power. By maintaining all conditioning at the power end of the muscular fitness spectrum, power can be maintained or even increased throughout the competition phase (Rhea et al., 2008). In addition, Baker (2001) showed that strength and power developed in the pre-season phase could be maintained for long in-season periods of up to 29 weeks despite a reduction in strength training volume.

2.2.2. Periodization

The concept of dividing the training season into smaller periods/cycles was a universally accepted monopolistic concept until recent years. Specifically, periodization is a systematic planning tool that divides the training period into short, manageable periods molded around one or several competitive years. Each period/phase has specific goals and objectives that aim to bring about improvements in ability at the appropriate time and especially when the player must peak for competition. Periodization also considers the sequential relationship between physical attributes. For example, one must improve maximum muscular strength in order to improve power. If the ultimate purpose of a training program is to develop muscular power, periodization allows logical sequence of biomotor development, which means muscular strength is initially trained and prepares players for ensuing power development (Bompa & Carrera, 2005).

Periodization is accomplished by manipulating the number of sets, repetitions or exercises performed; the amount or type of resistance used; the duration of rest between sets and or exercises; the type of contraction; or the training frequency between cycles. Because of the many variables that can be manipulated, there are numerous possible periodization programs (Rhea *et al.*, 2003). The classical Linear Periodization gradually increases the training intensity and decreases the training volume within and between the small cycles as the training program progresses. In contrast, Reverse Linear Periodization follows the modification in intensity and volume in reserve order as compared with Linear Periodization, i.e. increase volume and decrease intensity. Furthermore, Undulating Periodization involves manipulation of training intensity and volume throughout the training cycles in a more frequent way, i.e. by changing the program biweekly. In addition, Rhea et al. (2003) altered both training intensity and training volume on a daily basis, a process called Daily Undulating Periodization. Some training models are shown to be superior to other models in improving physical qualities. For example, Reverse Linear Periodization increased muscular endurance by almost one-third above Linear Periodization and Daily Undulating Periodization (Rhea et al., 2003). While Linear Periodization induces greater effects on muscle mass and maximal strength gains as compared to Reverse Linear Periodization.

The increase in the time spent in competition in professional sports can cause insufficient training stimuli and recovery leading to negative training results (Issurin, 2008). In addition, the application of traditional periodization may fail to provide multiple peak performances at different intervals during the year. To cope with this incompatibility, Norris & Smith (2002) redefined periodization concept as a framework within and around which a coach and sports science team can formulate a specific program for specific situation. Since there is no single periodization plan that best suits badminton, the periodization is highly dependant on the individual and the situation. In addition, in racket sports in general, there is a lack of studies on training regimes and peaking strategies for optimal performance (Pyne, Mujika, & Reilly, 2009). However, Linear Periodization may be a good model to improve players' maximal strength and power; and Reverse Linear Periodization is suitable in improving muscular endurance. Moreover, toward the pre-competition or competition phase, high intensity interval running can be one of the strategies employed to improve players' aerobic capacity while maintaining other specific on-court training routine. This training modality (> 90% of maximal heart rate) showed improvement in maximal oxygen consumption with no negative interference effects on strength and leg power (McMillan, Helgerud, Macdonald, & Hoff, 2005).

2.2.3. Common Injuries and Prevention

In badminton, some injuries tend to be associated with the specific demands of the game which require frequent changes of direction, sudden acceleration, abrupt deceleration, and unilateral use of the arm that is involved in repetitive overhead shots. In addition, overuse injuries tend to dominate injury patterns in badminton and compared to most sports, players are more at risk during training (Jörgensen & Winge, 1990). Previous injury in players has also been shown to be linked to a higher risk of incurring a new injury (Yung, Chan, Wong, Cheuk, & Fong, 2007). A previous study showed that most badminton injuries occurred in the lower extremities (83%), and the upper extremities were 11% (Kroner *et al.*, 1990). Most injuries occurred in joints and were diagnosed as ligament sprain and ruptures (59%) while 20% of the players sustained a muscle injury.

The majority of badminton players experience patellofemoral pain syndrome and anterior knee pain when performing lunges to receive shots in the corner or jumping to hit overhead strokes. The multiple fast forward movements, sudden stops and backward movements as a result of fast changing between concentric and eccentric contractions of the knee extensor are the major causes of this syndrome (Jorgensen & Homich, 1994). Specifically, the change in direction causes the quadriceps to decelerate its eccentric contraction and the backward movement requires an abrupt concentric contraction in the same muscle. The repetitive change from eccentric contraction to concentric contraction and vise versa causes chronic overloading of the ligament and leads to painful sensations.

In badminton players, strains in the adductor groups of muscle of the thigh and the iliopsoas muscle have been frequently reported because of the necessity to perform deep lunging movements. These lunging movements involve severe eccentric contraction of the adductors and may be over-actively contracting the iliopsoas (F. H. Sanderson, 1981). In addition, Patellar Tendonitis, or jumper's knee, is caused by frequent eccentric contractions of quadriceps and landing on a hard surface (Bartllet, 1999). This pathology arises when the tendon/tissues surrounding the patellar become inflamed or irritated as a result of overused. The frequent changes in direction also overload the lateral ligament of the ankle, thus ankle sprains are also common in badminton.

Badminton players often incur overuse injuries in the trunk, and lower back pain. The rapid twisting and tilting movement of the trunk (F. H. Sanderson, 1981), and the focus of "shoulder-over-shoulder technique" to produce maximum force during overhead strokes lead to trunk injuries among professional badminton players. Furthermore, muscle imbalance is another reason for trunk injuries because the stronger side of the lower back would shift the body position and caused the weaker side to be in a constant stretch position- thus leading to painful sensations. In addition, increased lumbar lordoses caused by tight iliopsoas muscle, added extra load to the lower back (Jorgensen & Homich, 1994). Moreover, using the term "anatomy trains," Myers (2004) depicted the myofascial meridian in the human body suggesting that when a player uses one dominant arm frequently (right arm), the lower back at the non-dominant side (left) would suffer from overuse, eventually leading to pain or injury.

The shoulder joint is the most vulnerable joint and is prone to overuse injuries caused by repeated loading and excessive leverage force acting on the tissue (F. H. Sanderson, 1981). Indeed, specific badminton training including stretching and strengthening of the triceps surae and the muscles involved in the internal and external rotation of the shoulder and elbow during the badminton strokes is recommended (Jörgensen & Winge, 1990). Anterior shoulder muscle strain, usually the deltoids, are precipitated by fatigue in the players who possess incorrect overhead shot technique and attempt to smash too hard (Mills, 1977). Imbalance of the eccentrically activated external rotator cuff muscles against the concentrically activated internal rotator cuff muscles is the primary risk factor in glenohumeral joint injuries during overhead movements such as smashes (Niederbracht, Shim, Sloniger, Paternostro-Bayles, & Short, 2008). These demanding overhead movements also lead to shoulder impingement. This is a syndrome resulting from compression of the supraspinatus tendon, as well as the biceps tendon and subacromial bursa, between the humeral head and subacromial arch (Tokish, Krishnan, & Hawkins, 2004). Lateral humeral epicondylitis, on the other hand, is likely to be caused by excessive string tension, repeated loading and some powerful mishits (off-center hit on the racket), thus increasing the vibrations transmitted from the racket to the elbow of the players (Bartllet, 1999).

2.2.4. Strength Training Program Samples

Strength training is always considered as supplementary training to that undertaken on court. Strength training may be less important for the professional player who has already attained a satisfactory level of physical fitness notably in terms of strength and speed. In addition, workouts that are too intensive may interfere with coordination, a factor that is important in sports such as badminton in which high technical skills are required (Majumdar et al., 1997). Greater efficiency from training may be obtained by prioritizing other performance qualities as such technical, tactical, or mental skills development (Sturgess & Newton, 2008). Examples are provided in this section regarding youth/adolescent badminton players. However, they should not be considered as the only available training programmes for badminton because individualized aspects such as individual strengths/weaknesses, injury history, and biomechanical/anthropometric characteristics must be taken into account when designing the program.

In the sample program, some training exercises are presented which require fast movement speed (indicated as [plyo] in Figure 4). This kind of plyometric training focuses on the stimulation of the stretch-shortening cycle to enhance explosive performance (Potach & Chu, 2000). Moreover, several of the training exercises (indicated as [P] in Figure 4) emphasized the power output (force divided by time) instead of the work load. The rationale for these exercises is to train with the highest mechanical power output in order to induce the best enhancement in dynamic athletic performance (G. J. Wilson, Newton, Murphy, & Humphries, 1993). Specifically, it has been shown that training loads using 30-55% of 1 Repetition Maximum are optimal in producing the highest power output for upper-body multi-joint exercises; while 45-70% of 1 Repetition Maximum is optimal for lower-body multi-joint exercises (Kawamori & Haff, 2004). Furthermore, conditioning based on maximal power output is more suitable during the in-season because it improves the rate of force development and causes less muscle damage compared to strength training (Crewther, Cronin, & Keogh, 2006; Kawamori & Haff, 2004).

Phase: Pre-season general preparation Duration: 2 times a week for 5 weeks	
Exercise	Set x Intensity, Rest (sec)
Squat	3-4 x 8-12RM, 90-180
Multi-directional lunges	2-3 x 10-20RM, 90-180
Dumbbell or Barbell bench press	3-4 x 8-12RM, 90-180
Chin up or lat pull down	3-4 x 6-10RM, 90-180
Hamstring curls	3-4 x 8-12RM, 90-180
Shoulder press	3-4 x 8-12RM, 90-180
Leg press	3-4 x 8-12RM, 90-180

Biceps curls	3-4 x 8-12RM, 90-180
Triceps extension	3-4 x 8-12RM, 90-180
Wrist extension & flexion	3-4 x 12-20RM, 120
Floor crunch	3-4 x 12-20Rep, 60
Rotary torso	3-4 x 12-20Rep, 60
Back extension	3-4 x 12-20Rep, 60
Phase: Pre-season specific preparation Duration: 2 times a week for 4 weeks	
Exercise	Set x Intensity, Rest
Squat	3-5 x 5-8RM, 120-240
Dumbbell bench press	3-5 x 5-8RM, 120-240
Chin up	3-4 x 6-10RM, 90-180
Split lunges	3-4 x 16-20RM, 90-180
Box jumps [plyo]	3-4 x 8-12Rep, 90-180
Overhead cross-over	3-4 x 8-10RM, 90-180
Weight-loaded sit up	3-4 x 8-10Rep, 90-180
Medicine ball oblique pass [plyo]	3-4 x 16-20Rep, 90-180
Weight-loaded back extension	3-4 x 8-10Rep, 90-180
Phase: In-season competition Duration: once a week	
Exercise	Set x Intensity, Rest
Squat jump [p]	3-4 x 10-15Rep, 90-120
Bench press [p]	3-4 x 10-15Rep, 90-120
Chin up	3-4 x 6-10RM, 90-180
Weight-loaded split lunges	3-4 x 12-16RM, 90-120
Multi-box (i.e., 3 boxes) jumps [plyo]	3-4 x 9Rep, 120-240
Sit up medicine ball throw [plyo]	3-4 x 10-15Rep, 120-180
Alternate side back extension	3-4 x 12-16Rep, 90-120

Note: RM = repetition maximum, Rep = repetition, p = power exercise; plyo = plyometric exercise.

Figure 4. Strength and conditioning program for adolescent/youth badminton players.

Chapter 3

3. ROWING

3.1. PHYSIOLOGY AND BIOMECHANICS OF ROWING

3.1.1. Physical Requirements for Rowing

International rowing events are conducted over a 2000 meters racecourse. The time to cover this distance at the international level takes between approximately 320 and 460 seconds, depending on the boat category and competition classification (Ingham, Whyte, Jones, & Nevill, 2002). Boats are separated into two distinct categories; sweep rowing and sculling. Sweep rowing requires each competitor to row with just a single oar on one side of the boat. Scullers use two oars, each of which is shorter than sweep rowing oars, and pull on these simultaneously. Sweep boats are rowed by two, four, or eight person crews, with equal number of rowers pulling oars on the bow (left) side and stroke (right) side. Sculls are rowed in single, double and quadruple shells. Competition classifications are divided into a heavyweight or open category, where no bodyweight restrictions apply; and a lightweight category, where male and female rowers are held to maximum weight restrictions of 72.5 kg and 59 kg, respectively.

From a physiological point of view, the aerobic metabolism has been shown to contribute 67 - 88% of the energy requirement to row a 2000 meters race (F. C. Hagerman, 1984; Mäestu, Jürimäe, & Jürimäe, 2005; Mickelson & Hagerman, 1982; Pripstein, Rhodes, McKenzie, & Coutts, 1999). Rowing performance is highly correlated with absolute maximal oxygen uptake (F.C. Hagerman, 1994; Ingham et al., 2002). Considering the contribution of aerobic metabolism to performance, maximal oxygen uptake is a very important physiological parameter that should be assessed in rowers. The remaining 12 - 33% energy is derived from anaerobic metabolism, predominately through the lactic acid system with a smaller contribution from the alactic pathways (Mickelson & Hagerman, 1982; Pripstein et al., 1999). Therefore, measuring the anaerobic capacity of rowers during performance testing provides valuable information about a rower's physical abilities.

Several studies investigating the physiological characteristics of rowers have revealed that elite rowers have a greater value of maximal oxygen uptake than lower level rowers (Mikulic, Ruzic, & Oreb, 2007b; Secher, 1983). Indeed, physiological data from a heavy-weight rower who obtained seven medals in World Championships and Olympic Games showed that the ability of this rower to compete at top level for years was related to ability to maintain an outstanding maximal oxygen uptake (Mikulic, Ruzic, & Oreb, 2007a). Other investigations have also demonstrated a greater percentage of slow twitch muscle fibers (Roth, Hasart, Wolf, & Pansold, 1983), a higher lean body mass (Secher, 1983), and a higher maximal oxygen uptake at a blood lactate concentration of 4 $mmol \cdot L^{-1}$, in highly-skilled rowers (Mikulic et al., 2007b; Roth et al., 1983).

Muscular strength and power also play an important role in race performance, as rowers must repeatedly generate powerful strokes against the water to move the boat forward. Rowers are required to maintain an average force of 686 - 882 N for up to 210 - 240 continuous strokes over a 2000 meters race course (Ishiko, 1969). In a group of Dutch Olympic, national, and club-level heavyweight rowers of similar stature, international level rowers were found, on average, to exert a force of 2000 N in an isometric rowing simulation test whereas national and club-level rowers produced average forces of 1795 N and 1590 N, respectively. In general, the higher the competitive level of the rower, the greater is his/her strength in this isometric rowing simulation test as well as in other non-specific rowing tests such as an isometric arm pull and tasks of trunk flexion, leg extension, and back extension (Larsson & Forsberg, 1980).

3.1.2. Physical Characteristics

In addition to physiological and biomechanical factors, physique is an important element in rowing performance. Anthropometric data of elite rowers emphasize the importance of body mass and body size (Bourgois et al., 2001).

Rowing performance has been shown to be positively correlated with muscle mass and overall body mass in both junior (Barrett & Manning, 2004; Bourgois et al., 2001; Bourgois et al., 2000; Russell, Le Rossignol, & Sparrow, 1998) and senior (Hahn, 1990; Jürimäe, Mäestu, Jürimäe, & Pihl, 2000) heavyweight rowers. Successful rowers tend to be taller and heavier than other endurance athletes with larger absolute maximal oxygen uptake values (Steinacker, 1993). Among FISA (International Rowing Federation) champions, men were 10.0% taller and 27.2% heavier than the general Canadian population, and in women the differences were 6.8% and 18.7%, respectively (Shephard, 1986). However, if maximal oxygen uptake is related to bodyweight, rowers show relatively low values of approximately 70 $ml \cdot kg \cdot min^{-1}$ compared to other elite endurance athletes (Secher, 1993), and those with the highest absolute maximal oxygen uptake values tend to show the lowest relative maximal oxygen uptake values (Jensen, Secher, Fiskestrand, Christensen, & Lund, 1984). Research by Mikulic (2008) has shown that elite senior rowers (age 28.1±3.0 years) were taller than sub-elite senior (age 22.16±2.8 years) and junior rowers (17.6±0.4 years) by 5.4 and 5.1 centimeters, respectively, with senior elite rowers also possessing longer arm spans and leg lengths than the other groups.

Taller rowers tend to have longer limbs providing them with an advantage, for example, longer arms allow a more acute catch angle of the oar toward the stern of the boat and longer legs allow a longer drive of the oar in the water to the finish, resulting in a overall longer stroke (Steinacker, 1993). A longer stroke length has been linked with high level rowing performance (Ingham et al., 2002) and offers the rower a mechanical advantage over rowers with shorter limbs, because longer strokes mean the rower can accelerate the oar through the water over a longer distance for each stroke. Successful lightweight rowers tend to have a short sitting height plus longer upper and lower extremities (Rodriguez, 1986), allowing them to have long levers with less mass due to their shorter trunk height. However, to maximize rowing performance, it is also important to tune the rigging of the boat to match the rower's size and strength (Barrett & Manning, 2004).

Body mass values of elite senior rowers tend to be about 4.3 kilograms higher than sub-elite senior counterparts (Mikulic, 2008). A rower's body mass is supported by a sliding seat, so in principle, rowers do not have to support their bodyweight and can therefore afford to carry a greater body mass; giving larger individuals an advantage (Secher, 1983). As a result of the body mass being supported, rowers are not as disadvantaged as other endurance athletes such as runners, who are required to carry their own body weight, although body mass with high body fat content has shown to adversely affect 2000-meter ergometer rowing performance (Ingham et al., 2002; Secher, 1983). Therefore, while overall body mass is an advantage, the higher the lean to fat mass ratio, the more of an advantage the body mass is to the performer.

3.1.3. Body Movements, Muscle Recruitment and Range of Motion

The rowing stroke is a coordinated muscle action which must be carried out repetitively and with near maximal forces during a rowing race, yet must remain smooth force application in order to move the boat efficiently and effectively. The stroke can be divided into four distinct phases: the catch, the drive, the finish, and the recovery. These phases are examined below.

The Catch

Rowing is a cyclical action, so the catch may also be considered the last part of the recovery as much as it can be considered the first part of the drive. In the catch position, the blade of the oar is quickly placed into the water when the body is at the fully compressed position (maximal knee and hip flexion) as in Figure 5. Once the blade is locked into the water the rower apply pressure with the feet onto the fixed foot stretcher. By pressing on the foot stretcher the rower is able to apply forces through the body to the oar handle and in some respects, the rower is almost ‘hanging’ his bodyweight on the oar handles as he/she presses on the foot stretcher.

Figure 5. The Catch position just as the blade is locked into the water at full knee and hip flexion with maximal horizontal abduction of the shoulders.

The Drive

The first part of the drive after the blade is locked in the water at the catch requires maximum leg drive (Figure 6). The speed just after the catch is when the boat is at its slowest (Baudouin & Hawkins, 2002; B. Sanderson & Martindale, 1986; Soper & Hume, 2004). The more proficient the rower, the less he/she slows the boat down between strokes, requiring less effort to reaccelerate the boat. For fast boats, such as the eight, maximal quickness is more important than maximal force, because the boat is moving very fast. For the single, the boat is slower and therefore, more force can be applied. However, the force should be applied in such a way that the rower is not pushing the water with the oar, but is rather accelerating the boat past the oar that is 'fixed' in the water. The knees forcibly extend in the first portion of the drive by the action of the quadriceps and the feet are plantar flexed by the soleus and gastrocnemius muscles. At the same time, the hip extensors, gluteus, hamstrings, lumbosacral, and erector spinae muscles must also forcibly contract isometrically to stop the upper body from falling into flexion as a result of pressure on the foot stretcher. In rowing, not holding the back at the start of the catch leads to ineffective power transfer from the lower to the upper extremities through the kinetic chain (Nelson & Widule, 1983). In the middle part of the drive the trunk, which predominately contracts isometrically against the legs up to this point, then begins to extend forcefully with hip extension (gluteus and hamstring muscles) and with back extension (erector spinae muscles). The upper extremities also begin their pull by flexing the arms with the biceps, the brachialis, and the brachioradialis, whereas prior to this middle portion of the drive the arms were primarily in extension. In the final portion of the drive, the knees have reached maximal extension and extension of the hip and back are also coming to completion. While the hip and back are reaching full extension, the final pull with the arms is also made until the rower is lying back at approximately a 45 degree angle and the oar handles are brought to within a few inches of the ribs. At this point, the shoulder is extended and adducted, and the upper arm is internally rotated by the latissimus dorsi. The abdominal muscles (rectus abdominis, internal/external obliques) and the psoas muscles work to decelerate the body swing at the finish and prepare for changing the direction of the body after the finish (Mazzone, 1988).

Figure 6. The Drive portion of the stroke occurs by pressing with the legs against the foot stretcher, holding with the back, and pulling of the arms.

The Finish

At the end of the drive phase the oar is still in the water and the rower comes to the full 'back stop' position. The rower must then quickly tap downward pressure on the oar handle to extract the blade from the water and immediately continue into the 'finish' portion of the stroke as in Figure 7. The knees and ankles remain in the same position and the back extends a little more to allow clearance for the tapped downward oar handle; and the hands begin to move forward towards the feet. At this point, the recovery portion of the stroke commences. When the elbows are nearly at full extension, flexion then follows at the hip joint, while the knees and ankles remain in the extended position as in Figure 8. Once the hands have cleared the knees, and the trunk passes the vertical position by flexion of the abdominal and hip flexor muscles, the knees begin to flex, and the slide moves forward in a controlled manner towards the catch again.

The sequence of movements for sweep rowing and sculling are nearly identical, except in sweep rowing the trunk begins to rotate toward the oar side half-way into the recovery and maximal trunk rotation is achieved in the catch position. Therefore, sweep rowing incorporates more activity of the oblique muscles in comparison to sculling, which is a more bilaterally symmetrical activity.

Figure 7. Finish of the rowing stroke just after blades have been extracted and rotated or "feathered."

Figure 8. Recovery of the rowing stroke and moving towards the next Catch position.

Rowing is a repetitive action that requires a specific range of motion. Generally during the recovery phase in order for the knees and hips to flex maximally, the extensors of the hips, knees and ankles should be supple and relaxed. If the rower has poor flexibility of the hip extensors and knee flexors, such as tight or shortened hamstrings, tension within these muscles increase as the rower flexes forward at the hips and the rower compresses into flexion when moving towards the catch position, making the recovery phase less efficient. Furthermore, it is optimal for flexion of the hips to occur by tilting the pelvis anteriorly during the recovery phase as opposed to flexing at the lumbar spine, but the desired anterior pelvic motion can be restrained by the length and stiffness of the hamstring muscles. Shorter and tighter hamstrings are also associated with increases in lumbar and thoracic flexion (R. Gajdosik, Hatcher, & Whitesell, 1992; R. L. Gajdosik, Albert, & Mitman, 1994), which is not ideal for rowing posture and can result in sprains of the posterior ligaments and strains of the extensor muscles, as well as degeneration of the spinal joints (Segal, 1983). Rotational range of motion of the trunk is also important for sweep rowers, as they need to reach out over the gunnel of the boat to create a more acute catch angle. Therefore, flexibility around the hips, trunk, and shoulder regions are also necessary to ensure that the rower can smoothly lengthen out the catch angle.

With regards to enhancing flexibility, rowers can benefit from a flexibility routine, particularly of the legs, back, shoulders, and ankles (Reid & McNair, 2000). Continuous repetitive motions make some muscles naturally more flexible while others become tighter (Higgs & Mackinnon, 1995). Flexibility of the hamstrings, in particular, may be important, because in non-rowers associations have been made between low back pain and hamstring inflexibility (Biering-Sorensen, 1984; Halbertsma, Goeken, Hof, Groothoff, & Eisma, 2001). Reid and McNair (2000) suggested a link could exist between hamstring tightness and low back pain in rowers, but little research has been done on this area in rowers. As a general rule, in order for fluid motions to occur within the required joint range of motion for the rowing action, rowers should focus on stretching the quadriceps; hamstrings; iliotibial band; lateral hip flexors and rotators; lumbar paraspinals; psoas muscle; gastrocnemius, soleus, and Achilles tendon; thoracic flexors, extensors and rotators; rotator cuff; and wrist flexors.

3.2. Sport Specific Strength Training Programs

3.2.1. Modalities of Training Exercise

Aerobic fitness is a major determining factor in rowing, accounting for approximately 70 – 80% of performance (F.C. Hagerman, 1994; Mäestu et al., 2005). However, muscular strength and power also play a vital role in rowing. This is not only due to the impact that strength has on overall muscular endurance during a race, but power and strength also make an important contribution at the start of the race where the rower must accelerate a stationary boat as quickly as possible to attain race pace. Analyses show that the peak forces reached during the first 10 seconds of a men's singles race range from 1000 to 1500 N and peak power between 2500 - 3000 W, with peak force and peak power leveling off to 500 - 700 N and 1000 - 1600 W, respectively, during the middle of the race (Steinacker, 1993).

Strength training for rowers can be done in the gym, on an ergometer, or on the water. The main focus is to undertake resistance training to increase strength, lean body mass (for heavyweight rowers), and power. Lightweight rowers, on the other hand, may require strength training for maintenance of muscle mass and strength as they lose overall mass to make competition bodyweight. Rowers tend to focus on strength training in the gym early in the season when the intention is to increase muscle hypertrophy and base strength (Mazzone, 1988). As more time is spent on the water when the competitive season begins, less training may be done in the gym. This is when movement-specific power training on the ergometer should be increased and make up a larger part of the strength training regime.

3.2.2. Common Injuries and Prevention

The extreme physiological demands (muscular strength and aerobic endurance) on the rower make rowing one of the most physically challenging among all endurance sports (F.C. Hagerman, Hagerman, & Mickelson, 1979). Many strains from stamping down on the foot stretcher and pulling on the oar are consequently placed on the rower's trunk and lower back (Caldwell, McNair, & Williams, 2003; O'Kane, Teitz, & Lind, 2003; O'Sullivan, O'sullivan, A.M.J., & A.H., 2003; Reid & McNair, 2000; Roy et al., 1990; Teitz, O'Kane, Lind, & Hannafin, 2002). Research by Wilson, Gissane, Simms, and Gormley (in press) in senior international rowers has shown that the area where the greatest number of injuries were reported was the lumbar spine (31.82% of total injuries) followed by the knee (15.91% of total injuries) and the cervical spine (11.36% of total injuries). In international junior rowers, lower back injuries were also the most frequent complaint (Smoljanovic et al., in press). These back injuries can include spondylolysis, sacroiliac joint dysfunction and disc herniation (Rumball, Lebrun, Di Ciacca, & Orlando, 2005).

The trunk is considered the rower's central link in the kinetic chain, both transferring and generating forces from the legs (which press on the fixed foot stretcher) to the arms (which pull on the handle of the oar); actions which are critical to the propulsive force that must be generated to apply forces on the blade in the water (Baudouin & Hawkins, 2002). Consequently, the repetitive and high magnitude forces that are placed on the flexed lumbar spine contribute to low back pain in most rowers (Hickey, Fricker, & McDonald, 1997; Morris, Smith, Payne, Galloway, & Wark, 2000; Reid & McNair, 2000; Roy et al., 1990; Teitz et al., 2002; Timm, 1999). There are a number of factors related to the rowing stroke that are likely to increase the risk of low back pain. Hosea, Boland, McCarthy, and Kennedy (1989) reported compression loads on the spine as high as seven times body mass, with loads in the region of 3919 N for men and 3330 N for women reported during the rowing stroke. Rowers have also been shown to be in a flexed spinal posture for up to 70% of the stroke cycle and their spines are at 55% of maximum spinal flexion range, significantly increasing spinal compression and tensile stresses on the outer annulus of the inter-vertebral disc (Adams, McNally, Chinn, & Dolan, 1994). Additionally, Morris et al. (2000) also estimated peak forces at the lumbar spine to reach 2694 N and 660 N of compressive and shear forces, respectively, during a 2000 meters race simulation in female rowers. The cumulative effect of these loads on the spine is substantial over the race, where the rowing stroke can be repeated as many as 250 times. Moreover, in a single training session of 90 minutes, a rower may cover distances of over 20 - 25 kilometers, which amount to around 1800 cycles of flexion/extension per session. In addition, high training loads carried out on a rowing ergometer were significantly associated with injury risk in international rowers (F. Wilson, Gissane, Simms, & J., in press).

Rib stress fractures account for the most time lost from on-water training and competition although the exact aetiology of these fractures remains unknown (Rumball et al., 2005). Stress fractures to the ribs may be due to rib cage loading which generates bone strain in individual ribs (Karlson, 1998; Warden, Gutschlag, Wajswelner, & Crossley, 2002). Finally, other injuries which are specific to the ribs include costochondritis, costovertebral joint subluxation and intercostal muscle strains (Rumball et al., 2005).

3.2.3. Periodization and Strength Training Program Samples

Off-Season General Preparation Strength Training

The winter season is primarily the time when long distance rowing and strength training are emphasized. The strength training is divided generally into 3 phases, the hypertrophy phase, basic strength phase, and muscle endurance phase (Mazzone, 1988). During the hypertrophy phase, the rowers do strength specific exercises such as the leg press, dead lift, and bent over rows (or bench pulls), generally using 3 - 4 sets of 8 - 15 repetitions (Baechle, Earle, & Wathen, 2008). Figure 9 shows an example of hypertrophy training in this training period. In order to increase the volume of strength training without risking overtraining of certain muscle groups, a four day split routine may be incorporated into the training program. This allows the rower to work on most of the basic exercises at least twice per week for each muscle group. The split routine allows rest of some muscle groups, while still allowing the rower to carry out strength training of other muscle groups.

Phase: Off-season general preparation strength training **Duration: 4 times a week for 5 weeks (split routine)**			
Exercises (days 1 and 4)	Sets x Intensity, Rest (sec)	Exercises (days 2 and 5)	Sets x Intensity, Rest (sec)
Dead lift	3-4 x 8-12RM, 90-180	Chin up	3-4 x 8-12RM, 90-120
Squat	3-4 x 8-12RM, 90-180	Barbell bench pull	3-4 x 8-12RM, 90-120
Leg press	3 x 8-12RM, 90-180	Dips	3 x 12-15RM, 90
Good morning exercise	3 x 10-15RM, 90-120	Cable triceps press down	3 x 10-15RM, 90-120
Hamstring curls	3 x 10-12RM, 90-120	Rotary torso machine	3 x 10-12RM, 90-120
Bench or Chest press	3-4 x 8-12RM, 90-180	Side bridges	3-4 x 60-120sec, 60
Shoulder press	3-4 x 8-12RM, 90-180	Dumbbell side bends	3 x 8-12RM, 90
Bicep curls	3-4 x 8-12RM, 90-180	Hanging leg raises	3 x 8-12RM, 90-120
Incline Sit ups	3 x 15-20 Rep, 90	*Flexibility training*	
Front bridge	3-4 x 60-120sec, 60	Single leg hamstring stretch	3 x 30 seconds each side
Floor crunches	3 x 20-25Rep, 60	Standing toe touch	3 x 60 second hold
Lying leg rotations	3-4 x 20 Rep, 60	McKenzie stretch	3 x 20 Rep, 60
Back extension	3-4 x 12-20 Rep, 60	Lying torso rotations	2 x 30 seconds each side

Note: RM = repetition maximum, Rep = repetition.

Figure 9. Off-season general preparation strength training.

Pre-Season Specific Training for Power-Endurance

During this phase rowers continue to follow strength training programs, although less frequently than in the off-season. By carrying out power training in the gym twice per week, more time is allowed to devote to rowing specific training, which is still primarily endurance based training on the water and on the ergometer, with increasing amounts of anaerobic interval bursts and powerful strokes of 1 - 3 minute durations.

Phase: Pre-season specific preparation for power Duration: 2 times a week for 4 weeks	
Exercise	Sets x Intensity, Rest (sec)
Power clean [P]	3-5 x 4-7RM, 120-240
Dead lift	3-5 x 5-8RM, 120-240
Squat [P]	3-4 x 6-10RM, 90-180
Chin up	3-4 x 16-20RM, 90-180
Walking lunges	3-4 x 20-30 steps in total, 90-180
Bench pull [P]	3-4 x 8-10RM, 90-180
Dips (weighted or non-weighted)	3-4 x 8-10 Rep, 90-180
Lying leg raises	3-4 x 20 Rep, 90-180
Back extensions (weighted or non-weighted)	3 x 15-20 Rep, 90-180

Note: RM = repetition maximum; Rep = repetition.

Figure 10. Pre-season specific preparation for power. This phase builds upon previous strength phase with more emphasis now on attempting to move heavier loads faster, indicated by [P].

In-Season Competition Phase Strength Training

In this phase, the rower must prepare themselves for competition and the amount of time dedicated to strength training is often minimal (Figure 11). The rower may continue strength training once per week in order to maintain strength, but little focus is spent on trying to increase strength levels. Also during this phase, the rower will continue with exercises to help reduce chance of injury. These include continued strengthening of the trunk muscles as well as regular flexibility exercises. Tse, McManus, and Masters (2005) suggested that training of the trunk muscles might be beneficial in yielding improvements in trunk muscle endurance, which might also assist in preventing and reducing episodes of low back pain. As previously mentioned, strength and power contribute greatly to propelling the boat, but contrary to what is commonly thought, evidence suggests that trunk muscle endurance, not strength, is related to reduced symptoms of low back pain (Biering-Sorensen, 1984).

Phase: In-season competition phase strength training Duration: once a week for maintenance	
Exercise	Set x Intensity, Rest
Power pull	3-4 x 10-12 Rep with 40-50% of 1RM load (fast), 90-180
Leg press	4-5 x 6-8RM, 90-120
Bench pull	3-4 x 10-15RM, 90-120
Push up	3 x 12-15 Rep, 90-120
Rowing ergometer	5 x 20 Rep max effort at 20 reps per minute, 45-75
Back extension	3-4 x 10-15 Rep, 90-120
Lying leg raises	3-4 x 15-20 Rep, 90-120

Note: RM = repetition maximum; Rep = repetition.

Figure 11. In-season competition phase strength training. Focus is on maintenance of strength so that rowing specific training can be concentrated on without losing strength base.

REFERENCES

Adams, M. A., McNally, D. S., Chinn, H., & Dolan, P. (1994). Posture and the compressive strength of the lumbar spine. *Clinical Biomechanics, 9*, 5-14.

Andersen, L. L., Larsson, B., Overgaard, H., & Aagaard, P. (2007). Torque-velocity characteristics and contractile rate of force development in elite badminton players. *European Journal of Sport Science, 7*(3), 127-134.

Araragi, K., Omori, M., & Iwata, H. (1999). Work intensity of women competing in official badminton championship games: Estimation of heart rate during games in Japanese Intercollegiate Tournaments. . *Journal of Education and Health Science., 44*(4), 644-658.

Arnason, A., Sigurdsson, S. B., Gudmundsson, A., Holme, I., Engebretsen, L., & Bahr, R. (2004). Risk factors for injuries in football. *American Journal of Sports Medicine, 32*(1 suppl), 5S-16S.

Baechle, T. R., Earle, R. W., & Wathen, D. (2000). Resistance training. In T. R. Baechel & R. W. Earle (Eds.), *Essentials of Strength Training and Conditioning* (2nd ed., pp. 395-426). Champaign, USA: Human Kinetics.

Baechle, T. R., Earle, R. W., & Wathen, D. (2008). Resistance Training. In T. R. Baechel & R. W. Earle (Eds.), *Essentials of Strength Training and Conditioning* (3rd ed., pp. 382-412). Champaign, USA: Human Kinetics.

Bahamonde, R. E. (2000). Change in angular momentum during the tennis serve. *Journal of Sports Sciences, 18*, 579-592.

Baker, D. (2001). The effect of an in-season of concurrent training on the maintenance of maximal strength and power in professional and college-ages rugby league football players. *Journal of Strength and Conditioning Research, 15*(2), 172-177.

Barrett, R. S., & Manning, J. M. (2004). Relationships between rigging set-up, anthropometry, physical capacity, rowing kinematics and rowing performance. *Sports Biomechanics, 3*(2), 221-235.

Bartllet, R. (1999). *Sports Biomechanics: Reducing injury and improving performance.* . London: E & FN Spon.

Bartllet, R. (2000). Principles of throwing. In V. Zatsiorsky (Ed.), *Biomechanics in sports: Performance enhancement and injury prevention.* (pp. 487-504). London: Blackwell Science.

Baudouin, A., & Hawkins, D. (2002). A biomechanical review of factors affecting rowing performance. *British Journal of Sports Medicine, 36*(6), 396-402; discussion 402.

Bell, G., Syrotuik, D., Socha, T., Maclean, I., & Quinney, H. A. (1997). Effect of strength training and concurrent strength training and endurance training on strength, testosterone, and cortisol. *Journal of Strength and Conditioning Research, 11*(1), 57-64.

Biering-Sorensen, F. (1984). Physical measurements as Risk Indicators for Low Back Trouble Over a One-Year Period. *Spine, 9*(2), 106-119.

Bishop, D., Jenkins, D. G., Mackinnon, L. T., McEniery, M., & Carey, M. F. (1999). The effects of strength training on endurance performance and muscle characteristics. *Medicine And Science In Sports And Exercise, 31*(6), 886-891.

Bompa, T. O., & Carrera, M. C. (2005). *Periodization Training for Sports: Science-based Strength and Conditioning Plans for 20 Sports.* Champaign, IL: Human Kinetics.

Bosquet, L., Montpetit, J., Arvisais, D., & Mujika, I. (2007). Effects of tapering on performance: A meta-analysis. *Medicine And Science In Sports And Exercise, 39*(8), 1358-1365.

Bourgois, J., Claessens, A. L., Janssens, M., Van Renterghem, B., Loos, R., Thomis, M., et al. (2001). Anthropometric characteristics of elite female junior rowers. *Journal of Sports Science, 19*(3), 195-202.

Bourgois, J., Claessens, A. L., Vrijens, J., Philippaerts, R., Van Renterghem, B., Thomis, M., et al. (2000). Anthropometric characteristics of elite male junior rowers. *British Journal of Sports Medicine, 34*(3), 213-216; discussion 216-217.

Bradley, P. S., Sheldon, W., Wooster, B., Olsen, P., Boanas, P., & Krustrup, P. (2009). High-intensity running in English FA Premier League soccer matches. *Journal of Sports Sciences, 27*(2), 159-168.

Caldwell, J. S., McNair, P. J., & Williams, M. (2003). The effects of repetitive motion on lumbar flexion and erector spinae muscle activity in rowers. *Clinical Biomechanics, 18*(8), 705-711.

Capranica, L., Tessitore, A., Guidetti, L., & Figura, F. (2001). Heart rate and match analysis in pre-pubescent soccer players. *Journal of Sports Sciences, 19*(6), 379-384.

Carling, C., Bloomfield, J., Nelsen, L., & Reilly, T. (2008). The Role of Motion Analysis in Elite Soccer Contemporary Performance Measurement Techniques and Work Rate Data. *Sports Medicine, 38*(10), 839-862.

Carling, C., Le Gall, F., Reilly, T., & Williams, A. M. (2009). Do anthropometric and fitness characteristics vary according to birth date distribution in elite youth academy soccer players? *Scandinavian journal of medicine & science in sports, 19*(1), 3-9.

Carling, C., Reilly, T., & Williams, A. M. (2008). *Performance Assessment for Field Sports*. New York: Routledge.

Carling, C., Williams, A. M., & Reilly, T. (2005). *The Handbook of Soccer Match Analysis*. London, UK: Routledge.

Castagna, C., D'Ottavio, S., & Abt, G. (2003). Activity profile of young soccer players during actual match play. *Journal of Strength & Conditioning Research, 17*(4), 775-780.

Cheetham, P. J., Rose, G. A., Hinrichs, R. N., Neal, R. J., Mottram, R. E., Hurrion, P. D., et al. (1998). *Comparison of kinematic sequence parameters between amateur and professional golfers.* . Paper presented at the World Scientific Congress of Golf.

Christmass, M. A., Dawson, B., Passeretto, P., & Arthur, P. G. (1999). A comparison of skeletal muscle oxygenation and fuel use in sustained continuous and intermittent exercise. *European Journal of Applied Physiology & Occupational Physiology, 80*(5), 423-435.

Christou, M., Smilios, I., Sotiropoulos, K., Volaklis, K., Pilianidis, T., & Tokmakidis, S. P. (2006). Effects of resistance training on the physical capacities of adolescent soccer players. *Journal Of Strength And Conditioning Research, 20*(4), 783-791.

Chromiak, J. A., & Mulvaney, D. R. (1990). A review: The effects of training for combined strength and endurance training on strength development. . *Journal of Applied Sport Science Research, 4*, 55-60.

Coutts, A., Reaburn, P., Piva, T. J., & Murphy, A. (2007). Changes in selected biochemical, muscular strength, power, and endurance measures during deliberate overreaching and tapering in rugby league players. *International Journal Of Sports Medicine, 28*(2), 116-124.

Coutts, A. J., Reaburn, P., Piva, T. J., & Rowsell, G. J. (2007). Monitoring for overreaching in rugby league players. *European Journal Of Applied Physiology, 99*(3), 313-324.

Cressey, E. M., West, C. A., Tiberio, D. P., Kraemer, W. J., & Maresh, C. M. (2007). The effects of ten weeks of lower-body unstable surface training on markers of athletic performance. *Journal Of Strength And Conditioning Research, 21*(2), 561-567.

Crewther, B., Cronin, J., & Keogh, J. (2006). Possible stimuli for strength and power adaptation - Acute metabolic responses. *Sports Medicine, 36*(1), 65-78.

Di Salvo, V., Baron, R., Tschan, H., Calderon Montero, F. J., Bachl, N., & Pigozzi, F. (2007). Performance characteristics according to playing position in elite soccer. *International Journal of Sports Medicine, 28*(3), 222-227.

Di Salvo, V., Benito, P. J., Calderon, F. J., Di Salvo, M., & Pigozz, F. (2008). Activity profile of elite goalkeepers during football match-play. *J Sports Med Phys Fitness, 48*(4), 443-446.

Docherty, D., & Sporer, B. (2000). A proposed model for examining the interference phenomenon between concurrent aerobic and strength training. *Sports Medicine, 30*(6), 385-394.

Dudley, G. A., & Fleck, S. J. (1987). Strength and endurance training: Are they mutually exclusive? *Sports Medicine, 4*, 79-85.

Dupont, G., Akakpo, K., & Berthoin, S. (2004). The effect of in-season, high-intensity interval training in soccer players. *Journal of Strength & Conditioning Research, 18*(3), 584-589.

Elliott, B. (2006). Biomechanics and tennis. *British Journal of Sports Medicine, 40*, 392-396.

Elliott, B. C. (2000). Hitting and kicking. . In V. Zatsiorsky (Ed.), *Biomechanics in sports: Performance enhancement and injury prevention.* (pp. 487-504). London: Blackwell Science.

Elliott, B. C., Baxter, K. G., & Besier, T. F. (1999). Internal rotation of the upper-arm segment during a stretch-shorten cycle movement. *Journal of Applied Biomechanics, 15*, 381-395.

Elliott, B. C., Marshall, R., & Noffal, G. (1995). The role of upper limb segment rotations in the development of racket-head speed in the squash forehand. *Journal of Sports Sciences, 14*, 159-165.

Eygendaal, D., Rahussen, F. T. G., & Diercks, R. L. (2007). Biomechanics of the elbow joint in tennis players and relation to pathology. *British Journal of Sports Medicine, 41*, 820-823.

Faccini, P., & Dal Monte, A. (1996). Physiologic demands of badminton match play. *American Journal of Sports Medicine, 24*(6), 64-66.

Faigenbaum, A. D., McFarland, J. E., Keiper, F. B., Tevlin, W., Ratamess, N. A., Kang, J., et al. (2007). Effects of a short-term plyometric and resistance training program on fitness performance in boys age 12 to 15 years. *Journal Of Sports Science And Medicine, 6*(4), 519-525.

Fatouros, I. S., Jamurtas, A. Z., Leontsini, D., Taxildaris, K., Aggelousis, N., Kostopoulos, N., et al. (2000). Evaluation of Plyometric Exercise Training, Weight Training, and Their Combination on Vertical Jumping Performance and Leg Strength. . *Journal of Strength and Conditioning Research, 14*(4), 470-476.

Faude, O., Meyer, T., Rosenberger, F., Fried, M., Huber, G., & Kindermann, W. (2007). Physiological characteristics of badminton match play. *European Journal of Applied Physiology, 100*(4), 479-485.

Fleck, S. J., & Kraemer, W. J. (2004). *Designing resistance training program.* Champaign, IL: Human Kinetics.

Gajdosik, R., Hatcher, C., & Whitesell, S. (1992). Influence of short hamstring muscles on the pelvis and lumbar spine in standing and during the toe touch test. *Clinical Biomechanics, 7*, 38-42.

Gajdosik, R. L., Albert, C. R., & Mitman, J. J. (1994). Influence of hamstring length on the standing position and flexion range of motion of the pelvic angle, lumbar angle, and thoracic angle. *Journal of Orthopaedic and Sports Physical Therapy, 20*(4), 213-219.

Gambetta, V. (2007). *Athletic development: The art & science of functional sports conditioning.* . IL: Human Kinetics.

Gamble, P. (2006). Periodization of training for team sport athletes. *Strength and Conditioning Journal, 28*, 55-56.

Girard, O., & Millet, G. P. (2008). Neuromuscular fatigue in racquet sports. *Neurologic Clincs, 26*, 181-194.

Gorostiaga, E. M., Izquierdo, M., Ruesta, M., Iribarren, J., Gonzalez-Badillo, J. J., & Ibanez, J. (2004). Strength training effects on physical performance and serum hormones in young soccer players. *European Journal Of Applied Physiology, 91*(5-6), 698-707.

Hägglund, M., Waldén, M., & Ekstrand, J. (2006). Previous injury as a risk factor for injury in elite football: a prospective study over two consecutive seasons. *British Journal of Sports Medicine, 40*(9), 767-772.

Hagerman, F. C. (1984). Applied physiology of rowing. *Sports Medicine, 1*(4), 303-326.

Hagerman, F. C. (1994). Physiology and Nutrition for Rowing. In D. R. Lamb, H. G. Knuttgen & R. Murray (Eds.), *Perspectives in Exercise Science and Sports Medicine: Physiology and Nutrition for Competitive Sport*. Indianapolis: Cooper.

Hagerman, F. C., Hagerman, G. R., & Mickelson, T. C. (1979). Physiological profile of elite rowers. *The Physician and Sportsmedicine, 7*, 76-83.

Hahn, A. (1990). Identification and selection of talent in Australian rowing. *EXCEL, 6*, 5-11.

Halbertsma, J. P., Goeken, L. N., Hof, A. L., Groothoff, J. W., & Eisma, W. H. (2001). Extensibility and stiffness of the hamstrings in patients with nonspecific low back pain. *Arch Phys Med Rehabil, 82*(2), 232-238.

Halson, S. L., & Jeukendrup, A. E. (2004). Does Overtraining Exist? An analysis of overreaching and overtraining research. *Sports Medicine, 34*(14), 967-981.

Hamilton, N., Weimar, W., & Luttgens, K. (2008). *Kinesiology: Scientific basis of human motion.* New York: McGraw-Hill.

Hawkins, R. D., & Fuller, C. W. (1999). A prospective epidemiological study of injuries in four English professional football clubs. *British Journal of Sports Medicine, 33*, 196-203.

Heidt, R. S., Jr., Sweeterman, L. M., Carlonas, R. L., Traub, J. A., & Tekulve, F. X. (2000). Avoidance of soccer injuries with preseason conditioning. *American Journal of Sports Medicine, 28*(5), 659-662.

Helgerud, J., Engen, L. C., Wisloff, U., & Hoff, J. (2001). Aerobic endurance training improves soccer performance. *Medicine And Science In Sports And Exercise, 33*(11), 1925-1931.

Helsen, W. F., Hodges, N. J., Van Winckel, J., & Starkes, J. L. (2000). The roles of talent, physical precocity and practice in the development of soccer expertise. *Journal of Sports Sciences, 18*(9), 727-736.

Hennessy, L. C., & Watson, A. W. S. (1994). The interference effects of training for strength and endurance stimultaneously. *Journal of Strength and Conditioning Research, 8*(1), 12-19.

Hickey, G. J., Fricker, P. A., & McDonald, W. A. (1997). Injuries to elite rowers over a 10-yr period. *Medicine and Science in Sports and Exercise, 29*(12), 1567-1572.

Higgs, P. E., & Mackinnon, S. E. (1995). Repetitive motion injuries. *Annu Rev Med, 46*, 1-16.

Hirakawa, T., & Shogei, K. (1994). *Basic theory of badminton*. Taipei: Tohan Corporation.

Hoff, J. (2005). Training and testing physical capacities for elite soccer players. *Journal of Sports Sciences, 23*(6), 573-582.

Hoff, J., & Helgerud, J. (2004). Endurance and strength training for soccer players: physiological considerations. *Sports Medicine, 34*(3), 165-180.

Hosea, T., Boland, A., McCarthy, K., & Kennedy, T. (1989). *Rowing injuries. Postgraduate advances in sports medicine*: University of Pennsylvania: Forum Medicum Inc.

Ingham, S. A., Whyte, G. P., Jones, K., & Nevill, A. M. (2002). Determinants of 2,000 m rowing ergometer performance in elite rowers. *European Journal of Applied Physiology, 88*(3), 243-246.

Ishiko, T. (1969). Application of telemetry to sport activities. *Biomechanics, 1*, 138-146.

Issurin, V. (2008). Block periodization versus traditional training theory: a review. . *Journal of Sports Medicine and Physical Fitness, 48*(1), 65-75.

Jörgensen, U., & Winge, S. (1990). Injuries in badminton. *Sports Medicine, 10*(1), 59-64.

Jürimäe, J., Mäestu, J., Jürimäe, T., & Pihl, E. (2000). Prediction of rowing performance on single sculls from metabolic and anthropometric variables. *Journal of Human Movement Studies, 38*, 123-136.

Jensen, K., Secher, N. H., Fiskestrand, A., Christensen, N. J., & Lund, J. O. (1984). Influence of bodyweight on physiologic variables measured during maximal dynamic exercise. *Acta Physiologica Scandinavic, 212*, 39A.

Jones, A. M., & Carter, H. (2000). The effect of endurance training on parameters of aerobic fitness. *Sports Medicine, 29*(6), 373-386.

Jorgensen, U., & Homich, P. (1994). Injuries in badminton. In P. A. F. H. Renstrom (Ed.), *Clinical practice of sports injury prevention and care.* (pp. 475-485). London: Blackwell Scientific Publication.

Jullien, H., Bisch, C., Largouet, N., Manouvier, C., Carling, C. J., & Amiard, V. (2008). Does a short period of lower limb strength training improve performance in field-based tests of running and agility in young professional soccer players. *Journal of Strength and Conditioning Research, 22*(2), 404-411.

Junge, A., & Dvorak, J. (2004). Soccer injuries: a review on incidence and prevention. *Sports Medicine, 34*(13), 929-938.

Junge, A., Rosch, D., Peterson, L., Graf-Baumann, T., & Dvorak, J. (2002). Prevention of soccer injuries: a prospective intervention study in youth amateur players. *American Journal of Sports Medicine, 30*(5), 652-659.

Karlson, K. A. (1998). Rib stress fractures in elite rowers. A case series and proposed mechanism. *Am J Sports Med, 26*, 516-519.

Kawamori, N., & Haff, G. G. (2004). The optimal training load for the development of muscular power. *Journal Of Strength And Conditioning Research, 18*(3), 675-684.

Kellis, E., & Katis, A. (2007). Biomechanical characteristics and determinants of instep soccer kick. *Journal Of Sports Science And Medicine, 6*(2), 154-165.

Kelly, V. G., & Coutts, A. J. (2007). Planning and monitoring training loads during the competition phase in team sports. *Strength and Conditioning Journal, 29*(4), 2-7.

Kotzamanidis, C., Chatzopoulos, D., Michailidis, C., Papaiakovou, G., & Patikas, D. (2005). The effect of a combined high-intensity strength and speed training program on the running and jumping ability of soccer players. *Journal Of Strength And Conditioning Research, 19*(2), 369-375.

Kraemer, W. J., Patton, J. F., Gordon, S. E., Harman, E. A., Deschenes, M. R., Reynolds, K., et al. (1995). Compatibility of high-Intensity strength and endurance training on hormonal and skeletal-muscle adaptations. *Journal Of Applied Physiology, 78*(3), 976-989.

Kreighbaum, E., & Barthels, K. M. (1996). *Biomechanics: A Qualitative Approach for Studying Human Movement*. Boston: Allyn and Bacon.

Kroner, K., Schmidt, S. A., Nielsen, A. B., Yde, J., Jakobsen, B. W., Moller-Madsen, B., et al. (1990). Badminton injuries. *British Journal of Sports medicine, 24*, 169-172.

Kyrolainen, H., Avela, J., McBride, J. M., Koskinen, S., Andersen, J. L., Sipila, S., et al. (2005). Effects of power training on muscle structure and neuromuscular performance. *Scandinavian Journal of Medicine & Science in Sports, 15*(1), 58-64.

Larsson, L., & Forsberg, A. (1980). Morphological muscle characteristics in rowers. *Canadian Journal of Applied Sports Science, 5*(4), 239-244.

Le Gall, F., Carling, C., Williams, A. M., & Reilly, T. (In press,). Anthropometric and fitness characteristics of international, professional and amateur male graduate soccer players from an elite youth academy. *Journal of Science and Medicine in Sport.*

Lees, A. (2003). Science and Major racket sports: a review. . *Journal of Sports Sciences, 21*, 707-732.

Lees, A., & Nolan, L. (1998). The biomechanics of soccer: A review. *Journal of Sports Sciences, 16*, 211-234.

Liang, X. M. (1991). *Badminton basic technique and tactic*. China: Kwong Dong People Publisher.

Lo, D., & Stark, K. (1991). The badminton overhead shot. *National Strength and Conditioning Association Journal, 13*(4), 6-16.

Mäestu, J., Jürimäe, J., & Jürimäe, T. (2005). Monitoring of performance and training in rowing. *Sports Medicine, 35*(7), 597-617.

Majumdar, P., Khanna, G. L., Malik, V., Sachdeva, S., Arif, M., & Mandal, M. (1997). Physiological analysis to quantify training load in badminton. *British Journal of Sports Medicine, 31*(4), 342-345.

Malina, R. M., Eisenmann, J. C., Cumming, S. P., Ribeiro, B., & Aroso, J. (2004). Maturity-associated variation in the growth and functional capacities of youth football (soccer) players 13-15 years. *European Journal of Applied Physiology, 91*(5-6), 555-562.

Manolopoulos, E., Papadopoulos, C., Salonikidis, K., Katartzi, E., & Poluha, S. (2004). Strength training effects on physical conditioning and instep kick kinematics in young amateur soccer players during preseason. *Perceptual And Motor Skills, 99*(2), 701-710.

Manrique, D. C., & Gonzalez-Badillo, J. J. (2003). Analysis of the characteristic of competitive badminton. . *British journal of sports medicine,, 37*, 62-66.

Mashall, R. N., & Elliott, B. C. (2000). Long-axis oration: The missing link in proximal-to-distal segment sequencing. . *Journal of Sports Sciences, 18*, 247-254.

Mazzone, M. D. (1988). Kinesiology of the rowing stroke. *Strength and Conditioning Journal, 10*, 4-11.

McMillan, K., Helgerud, J., Macdonald, R., & Hoff, J. (2005). Physiological adaptations to soccer specific endurance training in professional youth soccer players. *British Journal of Sports Medicine, 39*(5), 273-277.

Mickelson, T. C., & Hagerman, F. C. (1982). Anaerobic threshold measurements of elite oarsmen. *Medicine and Science in Sports and Exercise, 14*(6), 440-444.

Mikesell, K. A., & Dudley, G. A. (1983). Influence Of Intense Endurance Training On Aerobic Power Of Competitive Distance Runners. *Medicine And Science In Sports And Exercise, 15*(2), 124-124.

Mikulic, P. (2008). Anthropometric and physiological profiles of rowers of varying ages and ranks. *Kinesiology, 40*, 80-88.

Mikulic, P., Ruzic, L., & Oreb, G. (2007a). What distinguishes the Olympic level heavyweight rowers from other internationally successful rowers? *Coll Antropol, 31*(3), 811-816.

Mikulic, P., Ruzic, L., & Oreb, G. (2007b). What distinguishes the Olympic level heavyweight rowers from other internationally successful rowers? . *Coll Antropol, 31*(3), 811-816.

Mills, R. (1977). Injuries in badminton. *British Journal of Sports Medicine, 11*, 51-53.

Mohr, M., Krustrup, P., & Bangsbo, J. (2003). Match Performance of high-standard soccer players with special reference to development of fatigue. *Journal of Sports Sciences, 21*, 519-528.

Morris, F. L., Smith, R. M., Payne, W. R., Galloway, M. A., & Wark, J. D. (2000). Compressive and shear force generated in the lumbar spine of female rowers. *International Journal of Sports Medicine, 21*(7), 518-523.

Mujika, I. (1998). The influence of training characteristics and tapering on the adaptation in highly trained individuals: A review. *International Journal Of Sports Medicine, 19*(7), 439-446.

Mujika, I., & Padilla, S. (2003). Scientific bases for precompetition tapering strategies. *Medicine And Science In Sports And Exercise, 35*(7), 1182-1187.

Myers, T. W. (2004). *Anatomy Trains: Myofascial Meridians for manual and movement therapists.* Churchill, Livingstone: Elsevier.

Nelson, W. N., & Widule, C. J. (1983). Kinematic analysis and efficiency estimate of intercollegiate female rowers. *Med Sci Sports Exerc, 15*(6), 535-541.

Niederbracht, Y., Shim, A. L., Sloniger, M. A., Paternostro-Bayles, M., & Short, T. (2008). Effect of shoulder injury prevention strength training program on eccentric external rotator muscle strength and glenohumeral joint imbalance in female overhead activity athletes. . *Journal of Strength and Conditioning Research, 22*(1), 140-145.

Norris, S. P., & Smith, D. J. (2002). Planning, periodization, and sequencing of training and competition: the rationale for a competency planned, optimally executed training and competition program, supported by multidisciplinary team. In M. Kellmann (Ed.), *Enhancing Recovery.* Champaign, IL: Human Kinetics.

Nunez, V. M., Da Silva-Grigoletto, M. E., Castillo, E. F., Poblador, M. S., & Lancho, J. L. (2008). Effects of training exercises for the development of strength and endurance in soccer. *Journal of Strength and Conditioning Research, 22*(2), 518-524.

O'Kane, J. W., Teitz, C. C., & Lind, B. K. (2003). Effect of pre-existing back pain on the indidence and deverity of nack pain in intercollegiate rowers. *The American Journal of Sports Medicine, 31*, 80-82.

O'Sullivan, F., O'sullivan, J., A.M.J., B., & A.H., M. (2003). Modelling multivariate biomechanical measurements of the spine during a rowing exercise. *Clinical Biomechanics, 18*, 488-493.

Owen, A. L., Wong, P., & Chamari, K. (In press). In-season weekly high-intensity training volume among professional English soccer players: a 20-week study. *Soccer Journal.*

Paavolainen, L., Hakkinen, K., Hamalainen, I., Nummela, A., & Rusko, H. (1999). Explosive-strength training improves 5-km running time by improving running economy and muscle power. *Journal Of Applied Physiology, 86*(5), 1527-1533.

Pelton, B. (1971). *Badminton.* New Jersey: Prentice Hall.

Plagenhoef, S. (1971). *Patterns of Human Motion.* Englewood Cliffs, NJ: Prentice-Hall.

Potach, D. H., & Chu, D. A. (2000). Plyometric training. In T. R. Baechel & R. W. Earle (Eds.), *Essentials of Strength Training and Conditioning* (2nd ed., pp. 427-470). Champaign, USA: Human Kinetics.

Pripstein, L. P., Rhodes, E. C., McKenzie, D. C., & Coutts, K. D. (1999). Aerobic and anaerobic energy during a 2-km race simulation in female rowers. *European Journal of Applied Physiology and Occupational Physiology, 79*(6), 491-494.

Putlur, P., Foster, C., Miskowski, J. A., Kane, M. K., Burton, S. E., Scheett, T. P., et al. (2004). Alteration of immune function in women collegiate soccer players and college students. *Journal Of Sports Science And Medicine, 3*(4), 234-243.

Putman, C. T., Xu, X., Gillies, E., MacLean, I. M., & Bell, G. J. (2004). Effects of strength, endurance and combined training on myosin heavy chain content and fibre-type distribution in humans. *European Journal Of Applied Physiology, 92*(4-5), 376-384.

Pyne, D. B., Mujika, I., & Reilly, T. (2009). Peaking for optimal performance: Research limitations and future directions. *Journal of Sports Sciences, 27*(3), 195-202.

Rambely, A. S., Wan Abas, W. A. B., & Yusof, M. S. (2005). *The analysis of the jumping smash in the game of badminton.* Paper presented at the XXIII International Symposium in Biomechanics in Sports, Beijing, China.

Rampinini, E., Coutts, A. J., Castagna, C., Sassi, R., & Impellizzeri, F. M. (2007). Variation in top level soccer match performance. *International Journal of Sports Medicine, 28*(12), 1018-1024.

Reid, D. A., & McNair, P. J. (2000). Factors contributing to low back pain in rowers. *British Journal of Sports Medicine, 34*(5), 321-322.

Reilly, T. (1990). The racquet sports. In T. Reilly, N. Secher, P. Snell & C. Williams (Eds.), *Physiology of sports* (pp. 337-369). London: E & FN Spon.

Reilly, T., Bangsbo, J., & Franks, A. (2000). Anthropometric and physiological predispositions for elite soccer. *Journal of Sports Sciences, 18*(9), 669-683.

Reilly, T., & Thomas, V. (1976). A motion analysis of work-rate in different positional roles in professional football match-play. *Journal of Human Movement Studies, 2*, 87-97.

Rhea, M. R., Oliverson, J. R., Marshall, G., Peterson, M. D., Kenn, J. G., & Ayllon, F. N. (2008). Noncompatibility of power and endurance training among college baseball players. *Journal of Strength and Conditioning Research, 22*(1), 230-234.

Rhea, M. R., Phillips, W. T., Burkett, L. N., Stone, W. J., Ball, S. D., Alvar, B. A., et al. (2003). A comparisopn of linear and daily undulating periodized programs with equated volume and intensity for local muscular endurance. . *Journal of Strength and Conditioning Research, 17*(1), 82-87.

Rienzi, E., Drust, B., Reilly, T., Carter, J. E., & Martin, A. (2000). Investigation of anthropometric and work-rate profiles of elite South American international soccer players. *Journal of Sports Medicine & Physical Fitness, 40*(2), 162-169.

Rodriguez, F. A. (1986). Physical structure of international lightweight rowers. In T. Reilley, J. Watkins & J. Borms (Eds.), *Kinanthropometry III* (pp. 255-261). London: E & FN Spon.

Ronnestad, B. R., Kvamme, N. H., Sunde, A., & Raastad, T. (2008). Short-term effects of strength and plyometric training on sprint and jump performance in professional soccer players. *Journal of Strength and Conditioning Research, 22*(3), 773-780.

Roper, P. (1985). *Badminton: the skills of the game*. Salisbury: The Crowood Press.

Roth, W., Hasart, E., Wolf, W., & Pansold, B. (1983). Untersuchungen zur Dynamik der Energiebereitstellung wahrend maximaler Mittelzeitausdauerbelastung. *Medizin-und-Sport, 23*, 107-114.

Rowbottom, D. G. (Ed.). (2000). *Periodization of training*. Philadelphia: Lippincott, Williams and Wilkins.

Roy, S. H., De Luca, C. J., Snyder-Mackler, L., Emley, M. S., Crenshaw, R. L., & Lyons, J. P. (1990). Fatigue, recovery, and low back pain in varsity rowers. *Medicine and Science in Sports and Exercise, 22*(4), 463-469.

Rumball, J. S., Lebrun, C. M., Di Ciacca, S. R., & Orlando, K. (2005). Rowing injuries. *Sports Med, 35*(6), 537-555.

Russell, A. P., Le Rossignol, P. F., & Sparrow, W. A. (1998). Prediction of elite schoolboy 2000m rowing ergometer performance from metabolic, anthropometric and strength variables. *Journal of Sports Science, 16*(8), 749-754.

Sakurai, S., & Ohtsuki, T. (2000). Muscle activity and accuracy of performance of the smash stroke in badminton with reference to skill and practice. *Journal of Sports Sciences, 18*, 901-914.

Sale, D. G., Macdougall, J. D., Jacobs, I., & Garner, S. (1990). Interaction Between Concurrent Strength And Endurance Training. *Journal Of Applied Physiology, 68*(1), 260-270.

Sanderson, B., & Martindale, W. (1986). Towards optimizing rowing technique. *Med Sci Sports Exerc, 18*(4), 454-468.

Sanderson, F. H. (1981). Injuries in racket sports. In T. Reilly (Ed.), *Sport Fitness and Sports Injuries* (pp. 175-182). London: Faber and Faber Limited.

Secher, N. H. (1983). The physiology of rowing. *Journal of Sports Science, 1*, 23-53.

Secher, N. H. (1993). Physiological and biomechanical aspects of rowing: implications for training. *Sports Medicine, 15*, 24-42.

Segal, D. D. (1983). An anatomic and biomechanic approach to low back health: A preventive approach. *journal of sports Medicine, 23*, 411-421.

Shephard, R. J. (1986). *Fitness of a nation: lessons from the Canada fitness survey.* (Vol. 22). Basel: Karger.

Sheppard, J. M., & Young, W. B. (2006). Agility literature review: Classifications, training and testing. *Journal of Sports Sciences, 24*(9), 919-932.

Smoljanovic, T., Bojanic, I., Hannafin, J. A., Hren, D., Delimar, D., & Pecina, M. (in press). Traumatic and Overuse Injuries Among International Elite Junior Rowers. *Am J Sports Med.*

Soper, C., & Hume, A. P. (2004). Towards an Ideal Rowing Technique for Performance. *Sports Medicine, 34*(12), 825-848.

Sprigings, E., Marshall, R., Elliott, B., & Jennings, L. (1994). A three-dimensional kinematic method for determining the effectiveness of arm segment rotations in producing racquet-head speed. *Journal of Biomechanics, 27*(3), 245-254.

Steinacker, J. M. (1993). Physiological aspects of training in rowing. *International Journal of Sports Medicine, 14 Suppl 1*, S3-10.

Stolen, T., Chamari, K., Castagna, C., & Wisloff, U. (2005). Physiology of soccer: an update. *Sports Medicine, 35*(6), 501-536.

Sturgess, S., & Newton, R. U. (2008). Design and implementation of a specific strength program for badminton. . *Strength and Conditioniong Journal, 30*(3), 33-41.

Tang, H. P., Abe, K., Katon, K., & Ae, M. (1995). Three dimensional cinematographic analysis of the badminton forehand smash: movements of the forearm and hand. In T. Reilly, M. Hughes & A. Lees (Eds.), *Science and Racket Sports* (pp. 113-120). London: E & FN Spon.

Teitz, C. C., O'Kane, J., Lind, B. K., & Hannafin, J. A. (2002). Back pain in intercollegiate rowers. *American Journal of Sports Medicine, 30*(5), 674-679.

Timm, K. E. (1999). Sacroiliac joint dysfunction in elite rowers. *Journal of Orthopaedic and Sports Physical Therapy, 29*(5), 288-293.

Tokish, J. M., Krishnan, S. G., & Hawkins, R. J. (2004). Clinical examination of the overhead athlete: The "differential-directed" approach. . In S. G. Krishnan, R. J. Hawkins & R. F. Warren (Eds.), *The shoulder and the overhead athlete*. US: Lippincott Williams & Wilkins.

Tomlin, D. L., & Wenger, H. A. (2001). The relationship between aerobic fitness and recovery from high intensity intermittent exercise. . *Sports Medicine, 31*(1), 1-11.

Tong, Y. M., & Hong, Y. (2000). *The playing pattern of world's top single badminton players* Paper presented at the XVIII International Symposium on Biomechanics in Sports, Hong Kong.

Tropp, H., Askling, C., & Gillguist, J. (1985). Prevention of ankle sprains. *American Journal of Sports Medicine, 13*(4), 259-262.

Tsai, C. L., & Chang, S. S. (1998). *Biomechanical analysis of differences in the badminton smash and jump smash between Taiwan elite and collegiate players.* Paper presented at the XVI International Symposium on Biomechanics in Sports., Germany.

Tse, M. A., McManus, A. M., & Masters, R. S. (2005). Development and validation of a core endurance intervention program: implications for performance in college-age rowers. *J Strength Cond Res, 19*(3), 547-552.

United States Olympic Committee. (1998). *A basic guide to badminton*: Griffin Publishing Group.

Waddell, D. B., & Gowitzke, B. A. (2000). *Biomechanical principles applied to badminton power strokes.* Paper presented at the XVIII International Symposium on Biomechanics in Sports, Hong Kong.

Wang, W. J. (1995). *China sports coaching: Post training teaching material: Badminton.* . Beijing, China: Ren Ming Ti Yu Publisher.

Warden, S. J., Gutschlag, F. R., Wajswelner, H., & Crossley, K. M. (2002). Aetiology of rib stress fractures in rowers. *Sports Medicine, 32*(13), 819-836.

Wathen, D., Baechel, T. R., & Earle, R. W. (2000). Training variation: periodization. In T. R. Baechel & R. W. Earle (Eds.), *Essentials of Strength Training and Conditioning* (2nd ed., pp. 513-528). Champaign, USA: Human Kinetics.

Wilson, F., Gissane, C., Simms, C., & Gormley, J. (in press). A 12 month prospective cohort study of injury in international rowers. *Br J Sports Med.*

Wilson, F., Gissane, C., Simms, C., & J., G. (in press). A 12 month prospective cohort study of injury in international rowers. *Br J Sports Med.*

Wilson, G. J., Newton, R. U., Murphy, A. J., & Humphries, B. J. (1993). The Optimal Training Load For The Development Of Dynamic Athletic Performance. *Medicine And Science In Sports And Exercise, 25*(11), 1279-1286.

Wisloff, U., Castagna, C., Helgerud, J., Jones, R., & Hoff, J. (2004). Strong correlation of maximal squat strength with sprint performance and vertical jump height in elite soccer players. *British Journal of Sports Medicine, 38*(3), 285-288.

Wong, P., Chamari, K., Dellal, A., & Wisloff, U. (In press). Relationship between anthropometric and physiological characteristics in youth soccer players. *Journal of Strength and Conditioning Research.*

Wong, P., Chamari, K., Moalla, W., Chaouachi, A., Luk, T. C., & Lau, P. W. C. (In press). Heart rate response and match repeated-sprint performance in Chinese elite youth soccer players. *Soccer Journal.*

Wong, P., Chamari, K., & Wisloff, U. (In press). Effects of 12-week on-field combined strength and power training on physical performance among U-14 young soccer players. *Journal of Strength and Conditioning Research.*

Wong, P., Chaouachi, A., Chamari, K., Dellal, A., & Wisloff, U. (In press). Effect of pre-season concurrent muscular strength and high-intensity interval training in professional soccer players. *Journal of Strength and Conditioning Research.*

Wong, P., & Hong, Y. (2005). Soccer injury in the lower extremities. *British Journal of Sports Medicine, 39*(8), 473-482.

Wong, P., Mujika, I., Castagna, C., Chamari, K., Lau, P. W. C., & Wisloff, U. (2008). Characteristics of World Cup Soccer Players. *Soccer Journal*(Jan-Feb), 57-62.

Wong, P., & Wong, S. H. S. (in press). Physiological profile of Asian elite youth soccer players. *Journal of Strength and Conditioning Research.*

Wonisch, M., Hofmann, P., Schwaberger, G., von Duvillard, S. P., & Klein, W. (2003). Validation of a field test for the non-invasive determination of badminton specific aerobic performance. *British Journal of Sports Medicine, 37*(2), 115-118.

Woodman, L., & Pyke, F. (1991). Periodisation of Australian Football Training. *Sports Coach, April-June*, 32-39.

Woods, C., Hawkins, R., Hulse, M., & Hodson, A. (2003). The Football Association Medical Research Programme: an audit of injuries in professional football: an analysis of ankle sprains *British Journal of Sports Medicine, 37*(3), 233-238.

Yung, P. S., Chan, R. H., Wong, F. C., Cheuk, P. W., & Fong, D. T. (2007). Epidemiology of injuries in Hong Kong elite badminton athletes. *Research in Sports Medicine, 15*(2), 133-146.

INDEX

D

E

F

G

H

I

J

K

L

M

N

O

P

Q

R

S

T

U

V

W